This book is a gift to

_____

From

_____

Date

_____

The Power of Prayer

© 2007 Christian Art Gifts, RSA
          Christian Art Gifts Inc., IL, USA

Designed by Christian Art Gifts

Compiled by Kobus Sandenbergh from *The Necessity of Prayer*, *Essentials of Prayer*, and *Power through Prayer* by E. M. Bounds

Printed in China

ISBN 978-1-86920-835-6

09 10 11 12 13 14 15 16 17 18 – 18 17 16 15 14 13 12 11 10 9

THE POWER OF
PRAYER

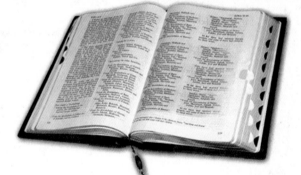

E. M. BOUNDS

christian
art gifts®

January

Wholeness through Prayer

*But whatever was to my profit I now
consider loss for the sake of Christ.*
Philippians 3:7

Prayer has to do with the whole being of a person. When a person prays, he does so with his whole nature. When he receives benefits in prayer, it involves his whole being.

The largest results of praying come to him who gives himself – all of himself, all that belongs to himself – to God.

This is the secret of full consecration and the sort of praying that produces the largest fruit.

Dear Lord, I want to give myself to You completely in prayer so that my life can produce the largest fruit for Your Glory. Amen.

January 1

Powerful Prayer

He will call upon Me, and I will answer him; I will be with him in trouble, I will deliver him and honor him.
Psalm 91:15

What are the possibilities of prayer according to divine revelation? The necessity of prayer is co-existent with man. Nature cries out in prayer.

Man is; therefore, prayer is. God is; therefore, prayer is. Prayer is born of the instincts, the needs, the cravings, and the very being of man.

God put no limitation on His ability to save through true praying. The possibilities of prayer are linked to the infinite righteousness and to the omnipotent power of God. There is nothing too hard for God to do.

Dear God, because all things are possible with You, I know that the possibilities of prayer are endless. All we have to do is ask. Amen.

Unite in Prayer

*May God Himself, the God of peace, sanctify you through
and through. May your whole spirit, soul and body
be kept blameless at the coming of our Lord Jesus Christ.*
1 Thessalonians 5:23

Holiness means wholeness. God wants holy people who are whole-hearted and true, for His service and for the work of praying. These are the sort of people God wants for leaders and these are the kind out of which the praying class is formed.

When a person prays every part of his being unites with God in prayer. Man unites in all the essentials and acts of piety. Soul, spirit, and body must unite in all things pertaining to life and godliness.

*Dear God, I want to be part of Your praying people.
Make me whole and holy for Your service. Amen.*

Kneeling to Pray

He withdrew about a stone's throw
beyond them, knelt down and prayed.
Luke 22:41

A person's body actively engages in prayer, since it assumes a specific position in prayer. Kneeling down of the body as well as the soul happens when someone prays. The attitude of the body counts much in prayer.

In Gethsemane our Lord prostrated Himself when He prayed just before His betrayal. Where there is earnest and faithful praying, the body always takes on the form most suited to the state of the soul at the time. In that way the body joins the soul in praying.

Almighty God, my soul is bent on pleasing You as my body kneels down before You in earnest prayer. Amen.

The Praying Mind

Do not conform any longer to the pattern of this world,
but be transformed by the renewing of your mind.
Then you will be able to test and approve what
God's will is – His good, pleasing and perfect will.
Romans 12:2

The whole being of a person must engage in prayer. A person's life, heart, temper and mind should be in it. Every fiber of a person should join in the prayer exercise.

A person's intellect must also add energy when praying. Necessarily the mind plays a role in prayer. First of all, one thinks about praying. The intellect teaches us that we ought to pray. By serious thinking beforehand, the mind prepares itself for approaching the throne of grace.

Thought precedes entering into prayer and prepares the way; it considers what will be asked in prayer.

Dear God, as I approach Your throne of grace I want to give my all to You – body, mind and soul. Amen.

Just Asking

"Lord, teach us to pray."
Luke 11:1

True praying involves knowing beforehand what to request from God. Praying is asking for something definite. The mind is given over entirely to God, thinking of Him, of what is needed, and of what has been received in the past.

The very first step in prayer is a mental step. We must be taught through our intellect. And only as far as the intellect is given over to God in prayer will we be able to learn how to pray.

Lord Jesus, just like Your disciples long ago I ask of You today, "teach us to pray." Amen.

Earnestness vs. Anointing

Faith is being sure of what we hope for
and certain of what we do not see.
Hebrews 11:1

Often, earnestness is mistaken for anointing. He who has the divine anointing will be earnest in the spiritual nature of things.

Earnestness may mean being sincere, serious, ardent, and persevering. But all these forces cannot rise higher than the mere human. The man is in it – the whole man, but God might not be in it. Earnestness could be selfishness in disguise.

What about the anointing? It is the indefinable aspect of preaching which makes it preaching. Anointing is that which distinguishes and separates preaching from all mere human speeches and presentations. It is the divine aspect in preaching.

Dear God, when I come to You in prayer I want to pray selflessly, and that by Your grace I may receive the anointing of Your Holy Spirit. Please guide me. Amen.

January 7

Far-Reaching Prayer

*Blessed are they who keep His statutes
and seek Him with all their heart.*
Psalm 119:2

It is godly people who give themselves entirely over to prayer. Prayer is far-reaching in its influence and in its gracious effects.

It is an intense and profound business that deals with God and His plans and purposes, and it takes whole-hearted people to do it.

No half-hearted, half-spirited effort will do for this all-important, heavenly business. The whole person must be engaged in the matter of praying which so mightily affects the characters and destinies of those who pray.

Dear Lord God, when I pray I know that no half-hearted, half-spirited effort will do. Please help me to surrender my all to You in prayer. Amen.

Today's Manna

*You will keep in perfect peace him whose mind
is steadfast, because he trusts in You.*
Isaiah 26:3

True prayers are born out of present trials and needs. Bread received today is the strongest pledge that there will be bread tomorrow. We must trust God today and leave tomorrow entirely with Him. The present is ours; the future belongs to God.

As every day demands its bread, so every day demands its prayer. No amount of praying done today will be sufficient for tomorrow's praying.

Today's manna is what we need; tomorrow God will see that our needs are supplied. This is the faith that God seeks to inspire. So leave tomorrow with its cares and troubles in God's hands.

Dear God, please help me to trust You for today's needs and to leave tomorrow entirely in Your hands. I know You will provide. Amen.

Praying Is not Child's Play

*During the days of Jesus' life on earth, He offered
up prayers and petitions with loud cries and tears
to the one who could save Him from death, and
He was heard because of His reverent submission.*
Hebrews 5:7

Praying is no light and trivial exercise. It engages all the powers of man's moral and spiritual nature as is evident in the Scripture verse above about the praying of our Lord.

It takes only a moment's thought to see how such praying drew mightily upon all the powers of God and called into effect every part of His nature. This is the kind of praying that brings the soul close to God and that brings God down to earth.

While children should be taught to pray early on, praying is no child's task. Prayer draws upon the whole nature of man – body, soul and spirit.

Dear Lord, thank You for Your example of what it really means to pray. Amen.

The Praying Christian

*I urge you, brothers, by our Lord Jesus Christ
and by the love of the Spirit, to join me
in my struggle by praying to God for me.*
Romans 15:30

Paul knew how to pray with his whole being. The words "to join me in my struggle" tell of Paul's praying and how much he put into it. It is like a great battle. Like a soldier, the praying Christian fights a life-and-death battle. His honor and eternal life are all at stake. Everything depends on the strength he puts in it.

Just as it involves every part of a person's complex being to pray successfully, so in turn the person receives the benefits of such praying. This kind of praying engages our undivided hearts, our full consent to be the Lord's.

Dear God, I want to thank You for knowing that when we pray to You with our whole being, You will bless our entire lives. Amen.

The Spirit's Gracious Touch

He makes me lie down in green pastures,
He leads me beside quiet waters, He restores my soul.
He guides me in paths of righteousness for His name's sake.
Psalm 23:2-3

God sees to it that when every part of a believer prays, He blesses that person. Clear thinking, an enlightened understanding, and safe reasoning powers come from praying.

Divine guidance means that God moves and impresses the mind in order for us to make wise decisions. Many praying preachers have been greatly helped and guided by God just at this point. In former days, when men of very limited education had such wonderful liberty of invigorated minds and thoughts from the Spirit, they explained it as successful prayer. Their minds felt the impulse of the Spirit's gracious influences.

Dear God, I pray that Your divine guidance will lead me in such a way that I too, will be able to experience the Spirit's gracious touch upon my life. Amen.

January 12

To Have Faith

"I tell you the truth, if anyone says to this mountain, 'Go, throw yourself into the sea,' and does not doubt in his heart but believes that what he says will happen, it will be done for him."
Mark 11:23

Faith is the essential quality in the heart of any believer who desires to communicate effectively with God.

He must believe and stretch out the hands of faith to that which cannot be seen. Prayer is faith claiming and taking hold of its natural, immeasurable inheritance. Moreover, when faith ceases to pray, it ceases to live.

Faith does the impossible because it lets God undertake for us, and nothing is impossible with God. How great – without qualification or limitation – is the power of faith!

Almighty God, I know that if I want to communicate with You effectively, faith is the essential quality. Thank You that the impossible is possible with You. Amen.

January 13

When Faith Fails

"Simon, Simon, Satan has asked to sift you as wheat. But I have prayed for you, Simon, that your faith may not fail. And when you have turned back, strengthen your brothers."
Luke 22:31-32

Faith is the foundation of a Christian character and the security of the soul. Here Jesus was looking toward Peter's denial and cautioning him against it. Our Lord was stating a central truth. It was Peter's faith He was seeking to guard.

He knew that when faith breaks down, the foundations of spiritual life give way too, and the entire structure of religious experience falls.

It was Peter's faith that needed guarding. That is why Christ was concerned for the welfare of His disciple's soul and was determined to strengthen Peter's faith through His own victorious prayer.

God, You know that when our faith fails, our spiritual lives give way. Please strengthen and guard my faith today so that my eyes will be fixed on You always. Amen.

Adding Grace to Grace

Make every effort to add to your faith goodness; and to goodness, knowledge; and to knowledge, self-control; and to self-control, perseverance; and to perseverance, godliness.
2 Peter 1:5-6

Growing in grace and fruitfulness is a measure of safety in the Christian life. Faith is the starting point, the basis of the other graces of the Spirit. To grow in grace depends on starting right.

There is a divine order and Peter was aware of it. He went on to say that we should give constant care to making our calling and election secure. This election is secured by adding to faith that which is done by constant, earnest praying.

Faith is kept alive by prayer. Every step in this adding of grace to grace is accompanied by prayer.

Dear God, I want to grow in grace and faith. Please guide me through Your Holy Spirit to strengthen my faith through constant prayer. Amen.

Powerful Praying

*Jesus came to them and said, "All authority
in heaven and on earth has been given to Me."*
Matthew 28:18

Faith that creates powerful praying is the faith that centers around a powerful Person. Faith in Christ's ability to *do* and to do *greatly*, is the faith that prays greatly.

It was because He wanted to inspire faith in His ability to *do* that Jesus left that last, great statement behind for us as a ringing challenge to our faith.

Faith is obedient. It goes when commanded, as did the nobleman who came to Jesus when his son was grievously sick. To do God's will is essential to true faith, and faith is necessary for absolute obedience.

Dear Lord, please help me to put my trust in You more every day so that my faith may increase to pray more effectively and powerfully to You. Amen.

Patient Faith

Be still before the LORD and wait patiently for Him.
Psalm 37:7

Faith often requires waiting patiently before God and being prepared to wait for His seeming delays in answering prayer. Faith does not grow disheartened because prayer is not immediately answered. It takes God at His word and lets Him take what time He chooses in fulfilling His purposes and in carrying out His work.

There is bound to be some delays and long days of waiting for true faith, but faith accepts the conditions. It knows there will be delays in answering prayer and regards such delays as times of testing where it is privileged to show that it is made of courage and perseverance.

Dear God, please help me to wait patiently for Your answers to my prayers. Thank You that because of my faith in You, I will not grow disheartened. Amen.

January 17

Spiritual Anointing

For the word of God is living and active. Sharper than any double-edged sword, it penetrates even to dividing soul and spirit, it judges the thoughts and attitudes of the heart.
Hebrews 4:12

Everyone knows what the freshness of the morning is like when orient pearls abound on every blade of grass. But who can describe it, much less produce it? Such is the mystery of spiritual anointing.

We know, but we cannot tell others what it is. We call it *unction* or *anointing*. Unction is a thing that you cannot manufacture or produce. It is this anointing which gives the words of the preacher such meaning, sharpness, and power, and which creates friction and stirs and revives many a dead congregation.

Spiritual anointing is in itself priceless beyond measure if you wish to edify believers and bring sinners to God.

Dear God, I need Your spiritual anointing on my life. I want to be a powerful witness to You. Amen.

Today's Fresh Bread

"Give us today our daily bread."
Matthew 6:11

Faith covers worldly as well as spiritual needs. Faith drives away anxiety and unnecessary worries about what you will eat, what you will drink and what you will wear. Faith brings great peace of mind and perfect peace of heart.

When we pray for our "daily bread", we are in fact shutting tomorrow out of our prayers. We do not look for tomorrow's grace or tomorrow's bread.

Those who pray best pray for today's, not tomorrow's needs. Our prayers for tomorrow's needs may be unnecessary because tomorrow might not exist at all!

Father God, I know that You will provide for Your children day by day. That is why I pray only for today's bread. Amen.

Praying Is No Easy Task

He answered: "'Love the Lord your God with all your heart
and with all your soul and with all your strength and
with all your mind'; and, 'Love your neighbor as yourself.'"
Luke 10:27

This was the answer of Jesus to the scribe as to what was the first and greatest commandment. In other words, the whole person must love God without reservation. Such a person is required to do the praying that God asks of His children.

Just as it requires a whole heart given to God to gladly and fully obey God's commandments, so it takes a whole heart to pray effectively. And because it requires the whole person to pray, praying is no easy task. Praying is far more than simply bending the knee and saying a few random words. Praying is divine.

Lord, I realize again today that prayer is no easy task. You ask all of me when I come to You in prayer. Please help me pray. Amen.

The Dedication of the Temple

"Now My eyes will be open and My ears attentive to the prayers offered in this place. I have chosen and consecrated this temple so that My Name may be there forever."
2 Chronicles 7:15-16

The prayer of Solomon at the dedication of the temple is the product of inspired wisdom and piety, and it gives a lucid and powerful view of prayer. National calamities, sins, damage to crops as well as individual needs such as sickness, pain and one's own sin are in this prayer.

For all these things, prayer is the one universal remedy. Prayer to God, pure praying, relieves dire situations because God can relieve when no one else can. Nothing is too difficult for God.

Almighty God, thank You that I know You can do all things and that You can relieve all the troubles in my life. I only have to pray earnestly to You. Amen.

A Growing Faith

*"Therefore I tell you, whatever you ask for in prayer,
believe that you have received it, and it will be yours."*
Mark 11:24

Prayer puts faith in God and moves God's hand in the world. Only God can move mountains, but faith and prayer move God. In the cursing of the fig tree, our Lord demonstrated His power. Following that, He went on to say that large powers were committed to faith and prayer, not to kill but to make alive.

A faith that makes things happen is described here. This faith is an awareness of God, an experienced communion, a fact.

Is faith growing or declining as the years go by? Does faith stand strong and firm as sin abounds and the love of many grows cold?

Lord, it is only You who can move mountains, but thank You that my faith and my prayers move You. I praise Your name. Amen.

Whole-Hearted Prayer

*May God Himself, the God of peace, sanctify you through
and through. May your whole spirit, soul and body be
kept blameless at the coming of our Lord Jesus Christ.*
1 Thessalonians 5:23

The people of olden times who were very successful in prayer, who made big things happen, who
moved God to do great things, were those who surrendered completely to God in their praying.

God requires complete devotion when we pray.
He requires whole-hearted people through whom
He can work out His purposes and plans concern-
ing all people.

No person with a divided allegiance to God, the
world, and self, can do the praying that is needed.

*Dear God, I surrender my life completely to You to-
day. I want to give all that I have to You in prayer.
Amen.*

January 23

Prayer for Times of Trouble

*"Call upon Me in the day of trouble;
I will deliver you, and you will honor Me."*
Psalm 50:15

The many statements in God's Word set forth the possibilities and far-reaching nature and effects of prayer.

Yet the range of prayer is as great as trouble, as universal as sorrow and as infinite as grief. And prayer can relieve all these evils that come to God's people. There is no tear that prayer cannot wipe away. There is no depression of spirit that it cannot elevate. There is no despair that it cannot dispel.

Prayer always brings God to our relief to bless and to aid, and it brings marvelous revelations of His power.

Lord God, I know that in this life we will have troubles. But thank You that we can know that we don't have to lose heart, because You have overcome this world. Amen.

Samuel, Man of Prayer

*As for me, far be it from me that I should
sin against the LORD by failing to pray for you.*
1 Samuel 12:23

Samuel stands out as one of the Old Testament men who had great influence with God through prayer. God could not deny him anything he asked for. Samuel's praying always affected God and moved God to do what would not have otherwise been done had he not prayed.

Samuel stands out as a striking illustration of the possibilities of prayer. Prayer was no strange exercise to Samuel. Through him and his praying, God's cause was brought out of its low, depressed condition. A great national revival began, of which David was one of its fruits.

God, thank You that You use ordinary people, equip them, and guide them to do great things for Your glory. Amen.

The School of Delay

*"I tell you the truth, we speak of what we know,
and we testify to what we have seen, but still
you people do not accept our testimony."*
John 3:11

Delay is often the test and the strength of faith;
yet faith gathers strength by waiting and praying.
Patience is learned best when waiting is required.
In some instances, delay is of the very nature of
prayer.

God has to do many things before He gives the
final answer. Things that are essential to the lasting
good of the person who is requesting the favor from
Him.

Fear not, Jesus will come. His delay will serve
to make His coming more richly blessed. Keep on
praying. Keep on waiting. He will come and will
not be late.

*D*ear God, I praise Your name and I thank You that
I can be sure of Your answers to my prayers. Even as I
wait, I know You will never be late. Amen.

The Divine Art of Preaching

They asked each other, "Were not our hearts
burning within us while He talked with us on
the road and opened the Scriptures to us?"
Luke 24:32

The preacher who has lost this anointing has lost the art of preaching.

Whatever other talents or abilities he may have and retain – the art of sermon making, the art of eloquence, the art of great, clear thinking, the art of pleasing an audience – he has lost the divine art of preaching. This anointing makes God's truth powerful and interesting; it draws, attracts, edifies, convicts and saves.

This same anointing vitalizes God's revealed truth and makes it life-giving. Just like God's truth spoken without this anointing is dead.

God, I pray for Your anointing on my life today so that I, too, can bring Your message to other people in a powerful way. Amen.

January 27

Praying in the Name of Jesus

"You may ask Me for anything in My name, and I will do it."
John 14:14

What a wonderful statement! What God will do in answer to prayer in His name! Faith in Christ is the basis of all working and all praying.

All wonderful works depend on wonderful praying, and all praying is done in the name of Jesus Christ. The amazing, simple lesson is to pray in the name of the Lord Jesus! All other conditions are of little value.

If Jesus dwells in your heart – if the flow of His life has replaced all of your life – then absolute obedience to Him is the inspiration and force of every movement of your life.

Lord, thank You that we may ask for anything in Your name, and You will do it. Amen.

The Energy of God

For Christ's love compels us, because we are
convinced that one died for all, and therefore all died.
2 Corinthians 5:14

Divine anointing is the feature that distinguishes true gospel preaching from all other methods of presenting the Truth. It supports revealed truth with all the energy of God.

Anointing is simply allowing God to be in His own Word and on His own people. It inspires and clarifies a person's intellect, gives insight and projects power. It gives the preacher heart-power which is greater than head-power.

Growth, fullness of thought, and simplicity of preaching are the fruits of this anointing.

Dear Lord Jesus, I pray for Your divine anointing to inspire my intellect, give me insight and reveal Your power through me. In Jesus' name I pray. Amen.

January 29

Godlike Sympathies

*For there is one God and one mediator between
God and men, the man Christ Jesus,
who gave Himself as a ransom for all men.*
1 Timothy 2:5-6

Paul knew that the nature of prayer is part of a person's being. It must be so. It takes the whole man to embrace in its godlike sympathies the entire race of man – the sorrows and the sins of all people.

It takes the whole man to run parallel with God's high will in saving mankind. It takes the whole man to stand with our Lord Jesus Christ as the Mediator between God and sinful people.

It takes a whole person to pray, until all the storms that agitate his soul are calmed to great tranquility.

Dear Lord Jesus I want to thank You that You came to be the Mediator between God and us. Thank You that You gave Yourself as a ransom for our sins. Amen.

The Gift of God

*Let us draw near to God with a sincere heart
in full assurance of faith, having our hearts
sprinkled to cleanse us from a guilty conscience and
having our bodies washed with pure water.*
Hebrews 10:22

This anointing comes to the preacher not in the study of God's Word, but in spending time with God. It is heaven's distillation in answer to prayer. It carries the Word like dynamite. It makes the hearer a culprit or a saint – makes him weep like a child and live like a giant.

It opens his heart and his purse as gently, yet as strongly as the spring opens the leaves. This anointing is not the gift of genius. It is the gift of God. It is heaven's knighthood given to the brave ones who have sought this anointed honor through many hours of prayer.

God, I draw near to You with a sincere heart. Please open my heart for Your divine gifts. In Jesus' name. Amen.

January 31

February

Prayer That Gets Results

"I tell you the truth, if anyone says to this mountain, 'Go, throw yourself into the sea,' and does not doubt in his heart but believes that what he says will happen, it will be done for him."
Mark 11:23

Genuine, authentic faith must be free of doubt. It is not a mere belief in the being, goodness and power of God – there's more to it than that. Through faith and prayer, God's promises will be done.

Our major concern is our faith – its growth and its tidings brought forth through its development. A faith that holds on to the very things it asks for, without doubt or fear.

We need this type of faith in our prayers.

Almighty God, I pray that You will grant me genuine, authentic faith which believes that anything is possible with You. Amen.

Being Sure

Faith is being sure of what we hope for
and certain of what we do not see.
Hebrews 11:1

Faith determines our relationship with God – how we deal with Him and how we see Him as the Savior. Faith grabs hold of the truth in God's Word and is energized and inspired by His holy fire.

God is the great objective of faith, for faith rests its whole weight on His Word. Faith is not an aimless act of the soul, but a looking to God and trusting in His promises. Faith is not believing just *anything*. It is believing God, resting in Him and trusting His Word.

Father God, it is my desire to be conscious of You all the time. Please increase my faith so that I will look to You and rest in Your promises. Amen.

A Life of Good Report

These were all commended for their faith, yet
none of them received what had been promised.
Hebrews 11:39

Today, many believers obtain a good report because
of their donations and their gifts and talents. But
there are few who obtain a good report because of
their great faith or great prayer life. Today, as much
as at any time, we need followers of God to have
great faith and powerful prayer.

These are the two most important virtues that
make men great in the eyes of God. These two
things create spiritual success in the life and work
of the church. It should be our main concern to see
that we keep this kind of quality faith before God.

Dear Lord, I want to live a life of good report. Please
help and guide me in developing a life of great faith and
prayer for Your glory. Amen.

Humility

For by the grace given me I say to every one of you:
Do not think of yourself more highly than you ought,
but rather think of yourself with sober judgment,
in accordance with the measure of faith God has given you.
Romans 12:3

Happy are those who have no goodness of their own to boast of. Humility flourishes in the soil of a true and deep sense of our own insignificance. Nowhere does humility flourish so as when it admits all guilt, confesses all sin, and trusts all grace.

"I the chief of sinners am, but Jesus died for me." That is the praying ground, the ground of humility, but in reality brought near by the blood of the Lord Jesus Christ. God dwells in the lowly places. He makes lowly places often the most high places to the praying soul.

Lord God, "I the chief of sinners am, but Jesus died for me." Thank You that we can know that when we humble ourselves before You, You will lift us up. Amen.

Twin Enemies of Faith

So do not throw away your confidence;
it will be richly rewarded.
Hebrews 10:35

Doubt and fear are the twin enemies of faith. Sometimes they actually take the place of faith, and although we continue to pray, it is a restless, disquieted, uneasy prayer that we offer. But doubts and fears should never be accommodated.

We must take our eyes off ourselves. They should be removed from our own weakness and allowed to rest fully on God's strength. A simple, confiding faith, living day by day, will drive fear away. Faith is able to cast your burdens onto God and not feel anxious about the outcome.

Dear Lord, doubt and fear often threaten our faith. I want to thank You for delivering us when we bring our weaknesses, doubts and fears before You in prayer. Amen.

February 5

Humility Gives
Wings to Prayer

Be completely humble and gentle;
be patient, bearing with one another in love.
Ephesians 4:2

Humility does not have its eyes on self, but rather on God and others. God puts a great price on humility of heart. That which brings the praying soul near to God is humility of heart. That which gives wings to prayer is a humble mind.

Pride, self-esteem, and self-praise effectually shut the door of prayer. Approach God with humility and meekness – do not be puffed up with self-importance or overestimate your virtues and good works. It is better to be clothed with humility than with an expensive garment.

Father God, You put a great price on humility. Please give me a humble and gentle heart so that my soul may draw ever closer to You. In Jesus' name. Amen.

The Divine Cure for Fear

Do not be anxious about anything,
but in everything, by prayer and petition,
with thanksgiving, present your requests to God.
Philippians 4:6

This Scripture verse describes the divine cure for all fear, anxiety, and worry. All these things are closely related to doubt and unbelief. This Scripture verse is also the divine prescription for securing the peace that surpasses all understanding and keeps the heart and mind in quietness and peace.

We need to guard against unbelief as we would against an enemy. Faith needs to be cultivated. Faith is increased by exercise; by being put to use. It is nourished by trials.

Faith grows by reading and meditating on the Word of God. Most of all, faith thrives in an atmosphere of prayer.

Dear Lord God, thank You that Your Word so clearly assures us that we need not worry or fear. You are always in control. Amen.

February 7

A Successful Pastor

In his pride the wicked does not seek Him;
in all his thoughts there is no room for God.
Psalm 10:4

It was said that Augustus Caesar found Rome a city of wood and left it a city of marble. The pastor who succeeds in changing his congregation from non-prayers, to prayer-filled people, has done a greater work than Augustus did. This is the major work of the preacher.

His main business is to turn people from being forgetful about God, into people who habitually pray, believe in God, and do His will. The preacher is not sent simply to get them to do better. He is sent to get them to pray, to trust God, and to keep their eyes on God.

God Almighty, I want to do great work for Your Kingdom. Thank You that I only need to plant a tiny seed; You will water it. Amen.

Saved and Sustained by Faith

For it is by grace you have been saved, through faith.
Ephesians 2:8

The work of the ministry is to change unbelieving sinners into praying, believing saints. The value of faith can not be disputed. God has placed tremendous importance and value on faith and that is why we need faith in order to be saved. So, when we think about the great importance of prayer, we find faith standing right beside it.

By faith we are saved, and by faith we *stay* saved. Prayer introduces us to a life of faith. Paul declared that the life he lived, he lived by faith in the Son of God who loved him and gave Himself for him. Therefore, Paul walked by faith and not by sight.

*D*ear God, thank You that I, like Paul, may also live a life of faith in Your Son who loves me and who gave Himself for my sins. Amen.

Faith's Inseparable Companion

Anyone who comes to Him must believe that He exists and that He rewards those who earnestly seek Him.
Hebrews 11:6

Prayer is absolutely dependent on faith. Prayer accomplishes nothing unless it is connected to faith. Faith makes prayer effective and must precede it.

Before we even start to pray, our faith should be working. We must have faith that God is a rewarder of those who diligently seek His face.

This is the primary step in praying. While faith does not bring the blessing, it puts prayer in a position to ask for it. It leads to another step of understanding by helping the petitioner believe that God is able and willing to bless.

Lord Jesus, without faith our prayers are without effect. Thank You that faith puts prayer in action. I praise Your name. Amen.

God Rewards

*"Your Father, who sees what is
done in secret, will reward you."*
Matthew 6:4

Faith opens the way for prayer to approach God.
But it also does more. It accompanies prayer with
every step. When requests are made to God, faith
turns the asking into obtaining. Prayer can help
build your faith, which will produce results.

Faith makes prayer strong and gives it patience
to wait on God. Faith believes that God rewards. No
truth is more clearly revealed and none is more encouraging in Scripture than this. Serving God – no
matter how insignificant it may seem – will yield a
reward. That is what faith whole-heartedly believes.
Faith gives its hearty consent to this precious truth.

*Father, thank You that even the most insignificant
service done in Your name will surely receive its reward. Glory to Your name. Amen.*

Do Not Grow Weary

I want men everywhere to lift up holy
hands in prayer, without anger or disputing.
1 Timothy 2:8

Doubting is always forbidden because it stands as an enemy to faith and hinders effective prayer. Paul gives us conditions for successful prayer.

All questioning must be guarded against and avoided. Faith must banish doubt.

Great incentives to prayer are furnished in Scripture. Our Lord closes His teaching about prayer with the assurance and promise of heaven. The presence of Jesus Christ in heaven and the preparation He is making there for His saints help us not to grow weary in prayer.

Lord, please drive away the doubts and fear in my life that hinders my prayers and threatens my faith. I ask this in Jesus' name. Amen.

The Spirit of a Pilgrim

But those who hope in the LORD will renew their strength.
They will soar on wings like eagles; they will run
and not grow weary, they will walk and not be faint.
Isaiah 40:31

The assurance that the Lord will come again to receive His saints strengthens and sweetens our difficult work on earth! To know that God is preparing a place for us in heaven is the star of hope to prayer. It is the wiping away of tears and putting the sweet odor of heaven into the bitterness of life.

The spirit of a pilgrim makes praying easier. An earthbound, earth-satisfied spirit cannot pray. The flame of spiritual desire in such a heart has gone out. The wings of its faith are clipped, its eyes are glazed over and its tongue is silenced. But they who wait continually upon the Lord *do* renew their strength!

God, I put my hope in You. Only You can sweeten the bitterness of life and change my tears to laughter. I wait on You; You will renew my strength. Amen.

Modesty

Honor one another above yourselves.
Romans 12:10

To be humble is to have a low estimate of oneself. Humility retires itself from the public gaze. It does not seek publicity, neither does it care for prominence. It never exalts itself in the eyes of others or even in the eyes of itself. Modesty is one of its most prominent characteristics.

In humility there is the total absence of pride, and it is far-removed from anything like self-conceit. There is no self-praise in humility. Rather, it has the disposition to praise others. It is willing to take the lowliest seat and prefers those places where it will be unnoticed. Humility is meek behavior, a submissive spirit and a modest heart.

Dear Father God, I know that it is only through Your grace I have been saved. Please grant me a submissive spirit and a modest heart. Amen.

Humility:
A Rare Christian Grace

Be completely humble and gentle;
be patient, bearing with one another in love.
Ephesians 4:2

Humility is a rare Christian grace of great price in the courts of heaven, and is necessary for effective prayer. It provides access to God when other qualities fail. Its full portrait is found only in the Lord Jesus Christ. Our prayers must be set low before they can ever rise high.

In our Lord's teaching humility has such prominence and is such a distinguishing feature of His character, that to leave it out of His lesson on prayer would be wrong. It would deny a very important aspect of God's character.

Dear Lord Jesus, I want to be more like You every day. Please grant me the rare Christian grace of humility so that everyone may see You in me. Amen.

A Praying Pharisee

"I tell you that this man, rather than the other, went home justified before God. For everyone who exalts himself will be humbled, and he who humbles himself will be exalted."
Luke 18:14

The parable of the Pharisee and tax collector stands out in such bold relief. The Pharisee seemed to be accustomed to prayer. Certainly he should have known by that time how to pray. He left business and business hours and walked with steady and fixed steps up to the house of prayer. The position and place were well chosen by him.

But this praying ecclesiastic, though schooled in prayer by training and by habit, does not really pray. Words are uttered by him, but words are not prayer. That season of temple going has had no worship in it whatsoever.

O Father, I don't want my prayers to be like that of the Pharisee. I want to come before Your throne with an honest and humble heart. Amen.

A Praying Tax Collector

"But the tax collector stood at a distance. He would not even look up to heaven, but beat his breast and said, 'God, have mercy on me, a sinner.'"
Luke 18:13

The tax collector, guilt-ridden with a deep sense of his wrong doings and his sinfulness, falls down with humiliation before God with cries for mercy. A sense of sin and of utter unworthiness have fixed the humility deep down in his soul. This is the picture of humility as opposed to pride in praying.

Here we see, by sharp contrast, the utter worthlessness of self-praise in praying. We see the beauty and the divine praise that comes to humility of heart, self-depreciation and self-condemnation when a soul comes before God in prayer.

Lord, I don't want to pray worthless prayers of self-praise. I pray with the tax collector, "God, have mercy on me, a sinner." Amen.

February 17

Humility Loves Obscurity

*This happened that we might not rely on ourselves
but on God. He has delivered us from such a deadly peril,
and He will deliver us. On Him we have set our hope.*
2 Corinthians 1:9-10

Humility is an indispensable requisite of true prayer. Humility must be in the praying character as light is in the sun.

Humility is born by looking at God and His holiness, and then looking at self and man's unholiness. Humility loves obscurity and silence, esteems the virtues of others, excuses their faults with mildness and easily pardons injuries. It knows and reveres the riches of the cross and the humiliations of Jesus Christ.

By approaching God's throne in humility of heart, a person will find comfort in knowing that God is all-powerful. Humility strives to be holy, like God is holy.

Dear God, please grant me the humility that is born by looking at You, and then recognizing my own sinfulness. Thank You for Your amazing grace. Amen.

The Pride of Doing

"Many will say to Me on that day, 'Lord, Lord, did we not prophesy in Your name, and in Your name drive out demons and perform many miracles?' Then I will tell them plainly, 'I never knew you. Away from Me, you evildoers!'"
Matthew 7:22-23

Humility is the first and last attribute of Christlike religion and the first and last attribute of Christlike praying. There is no Christ without humility.

How graceful and imperative does the attitude of humility become to us! Humility is an unchanging attitude of prayer. Pride sends its poison all through our praying. The same pride infects all our prayers, no matter how beautifully worded they may be.

This lack of humility, this self-applauding, kept the most religious man of Christ's day from being accepted by God. The same thing will keep us today from being accepted by God.

Dear Father, I know that my own pride and self-applauding can keep me away from You. Create in me a pure heart and renew a humble spirit within me. Amen.

February 19

Busy with the Business of Prayer

We will give our attention to prayer and the ministry of the Word.
Acts 6:4

The apostles knew the necessity and worth of prayer to their ministry. They knew that their high commission as apostles – instead of relieving them from the necessity of prayer – committed them to it even more.

They were exceedingly jealous when other important work exhausted their time and prevented them from praying as they ought. As a result, they appointed laymen to do the jobs that were distracting them from their prayer time.

Prayer is put first. They made a business of it, surrendering themselves to praying, putting fervor, urgency, perseverance and time into it.

God, I want to surrender myself to You in prayer by putting enthusiasm, perseverance and time into it. Amen.

Apostolic Praying

Night and day we pray most earnestly.
1 Thessalonians 3:10

The New Testament preachers laid themselves out in prayer for God's people. They put God in full force into churches by their praying.

The preacher who has never learned in the school of Christ the high and divine art of intercession for his people, will never learn the art of preaching. Though he may be the most gifted genius in sermon making and sermon delivery, he will never preach as the apostles, if he does not pray as they did.

Apostolic praying makes apostolic saints, and keeps apostolic times of purity and power in the church.

Dear Lord God, I want to pray night and day as Your apostles did. Please help me. Amen.

A Spiritual Energy

He has given us His very great and precious promises.
2 Peter 1:4

Without God's promise, prayer is eccentric and without foundation. It is prayer that makes the promises precious and practical.

Prayer as spiritual energy makes way for, and brings into practical realization, the promises of God.

God's promises cover all things that pertain to life and godliness and that have to do with time and eternity.

These promises bless the present and extend to the eternal future. Promises are God's golden fruit, to be plucked by the hand of prayer.

Father, I hold on to Your promises as I pray, so that I may pluck Your golden fruit of grace. Amen.

Humility That Energizes Prayer

*My heart is not proud, O LORD, my eyes
are not haughty; I do not concern myself with
great matters or things too wonderful for me.*
Psalm 131:1

Humility holds in its keeping the very life of prayer. Neither pride nor vanity can pray. It is a positive quality, a substantial force that energizes prayer. There is no power in prayer to ascend without it.

Humility springs from a lowly estimate of ourselves and of our deserving. To be clothed with humility is to be clothed with a praying garment.

Humility is realizing our unworthiness, the feeling and declaring of ourselves as sinners because we are sinners. Kneeling suits us very well as the physical posture of prayer because it speaks of humility.

Almighty God, I confess that I'm a sinner. Please forgive my sins and clothe me with a praying garment of humility. Amen.

Promising Prayer

Be joyful in hope, patient in affliction, faithful in prayer.
Romans 12:12

Prayer and God's promises are interdependent. The promise inspires and energizes prayer, but prayer locates the promise and gives it realization and location.

The promise is like the blessed rain falling in full showers. But prayer, like the pipes that direct the rain, focus these promises until they become direct and personal – until they bless, refresh, and fertilize.

Prayer takes hold of the promise and guides it to its marvelous end, removes the obstacles, and makes a highway for the promise to reach its glorious fulfillment.

Dear Lord God, thank You that our earnest prayers can put Your promises to bless and refresh in action. I praise Your name. Amen.

Elijah

"Go and present yourself to Ahab,
and I will send rain on the land."
1 Kings 18:1

Many glorious results marked that day of heroic faith and dauntless courage on Elijah's part. The happening on Mount Carmel had been successful, but there was no rain. The one thing, the only thing, that God had promised, had not been given.

Elijah turned from Israel to God and from Baal to the one Source of help for a final victory. But it was only until the seventh time that the promise was fulfilled.

Elijah's relentless praying bore to its triumphant results the promise of God, and rain descended in full showers.

Almighty God, please help me to pray relentlessly like Elijah did, so that Your glorious promises can be fulfilled. Amen.

February 25

The Prayer of Submission

You do not have, because you do not ask God.
James 4:2-3

Our prayers are too little and feeble to execute the purposes of God with appropriating power. Marvelous purposes need marvelous praying to execute them. How great, how sublime, and how exalted are the promises God makes to His people!

Prayer is based on the purpose and promise of God. Prayer is submission to God. Prayer is never disloyal to God. It may cry out in times of trouble, but it is rewarded with God's glory.

Father, I want my prayers to be based on Your purposes and promises. Please guide me. Amen.

According to God's Will

Being strengthened with all power according to His glorious might so that you may have great endurance and patience.
Colossians 1:11

Prayer is conscious conformity to God's will, based upon the direct promise of God's Word, and under the application of the Holy Spirit.

Nothing is surer than that the Word of God is the foundation of prayer. We pray just as we believe God's Word.

Prayer is based directly and specifically upon God's revealed promises in Christ Jesus. It has no other ground upon which to base its plea. Not our feelings, not our merits, not our works, but God's promise is the basis of faith and the solid ground of prayer.

Dear God, I base my prayers on Your revealed promises in Christ Jesus. Your Word is the foundation of my prayers. I praise Your holy name. Amen.

February 27

Chained by Prayer

"Therefore I tell you, whatever you ask for in prayer,
believe that you have received it, and it will be yours."
Mark 11:24

God's promises are dependent on our prayers. The promises are planted in us, appropriated by us, and held in the arms of faith by prayer. Prayer gives the promises their efficiency and utilizes them. Prayer puts the promises to practical and present uses.

Promises, like the rain, are general. Prayer embodies, precipitates, and locates them for personal use. The promises, like electricity, may sparkle and dazzle and yet remain useless for good until these dynamic, life-giving currents are chained by prayer and become mighty forces that move and bless.

Father God, thank You that our prayers can put Your promises to practical and present uses. All we have to do is believe in Your mighty name. Amen.

Answer to Prayer

"Ask ... seek ... knock ... it will be given to you ... you will find ... the door will be opened to you."
Matthew 7:7

Answered prayer brings praying out of the realm of dry, dead things and makes praying a thing of life and power. It is the answer to prayer that brings things to pass, and orders all things according to the will of God.

It is the answer to prayer that makes praying real. It is the answer to prayer that makes praying a power for God and for man, and makes praying real and divine.

Dear Lord, I want to thank You for answering our prayers. We must only ask and believe. You will answer in good time. Amen.

February 29

March

Wonderful Trust

"Do not let your hearts be troubled.
Trust in God; trust also in Me."
John 14:1

Prayer does not stand alone. It lives in fellowship with other Christian duties. Prayer is firmly joined to faith. Faith gives it color and tone, and secures its results.

Trust is faith accomplished. Trust is a conscious act, a fact of which we are aware. It is the feeling of the soul – the spiritual sight, hearing and taste.

All these have to do with trust. How bright, distinct, conscious, powerful, and scriptural such a trust is!

Dear God, I put my trust in You all day long. Amen.

March 1

Prayer Set on Fire

*Devote yourselves to prayer,
being watchful and thankful.*
Colossians 4:2

The Holy Spirit came as our promised Comforter, to help us in our prayer lives. The coming of the Holy Spirit is not conditioned on a little process and a mere performance of prayer, but on prayer set on fire by an unquenchable desire.

This prayer must be accompanied by such a sense of need that it cannot be denied, and by a fixed determination that will not let go and that will never fail until it secures the best and last blessing God has in store for us.

Dear Father, I thank You for sending us Your Holy Spirit to comfort us and guide our prayer lives. Amen.

Waiting in Mighty Prayer

"Woman, you have great faith! Your request is granted."
And her daughter was healed from that very hour.
Matthew 15:28

Trust brings eternity into the history and happenings of time. Trust sees, receives, holds. Trust is its own witness. But quite often, faith is too weak to obtain God's greatest good immediately. It has to wait in loving obedience, until it grows in strength and is able to bring down the eternal into the areas of experience and time.

Up to this point, trust is the deciding factor. In faith's struggle to grow stronger, trust also increases. If we trust in God, we will become more aware of all the good things that He has done for us.

While waiting in prayer, faith rises to its highest level and becomes the gift of God. It becomes a constant fellowship with a tireless request to God.

Almighty God, I know that if I trust in You, You will grant my requests. Thank You, Lord. Amen.

The Eye of Trust

*The Scripture says, "Anyone who trusts
in Him will never be put to shame."*
Romans 10:11

Trust grows richly when a person prays in solitude.
When a person's quiet time with God is sincere,
trust grows increasingly. The eye and the presence
of God give active life to trust, just like the eye and
presence of the sun make fruit and flowers grow.

Faith and trust in the Lord form the keynote and
foundation of prayer. Primarily, it is not trust in the
Word of God, but rather trust in the person of God.
For trust in the person of God must precede trust in
the Word of God.

The person of Jesus Christ must be central to the
eye of trust.

*Dear God, You are the central point of trust in my
life. Please make my trust grow as I come to You in
prayer. Amen.*

Believe without a Doubt

The apostles said to the Lord, "Increase our faith."
Luke 17:5

Do we believe without a doubt? When we pray, do we believe that we will receive the things we ask for, not on a future day, but then and there? This is not so easy. The ability to believe without doubting is only reached after many failures and much trial of faith.

Our Lord puts forth trust as the very foundation of praying. The background of prayer is trust. The whole purpose of Christ's ministry and work was dependent on absolute trust in His Father. The center of trust is God.

Mountains of difficulties and all other hindrances to prayer are moved out of the way by trust and its strong follower, faith.

Father God, thank You that You can move mountains if we only trust and believe in You. I praise Your holy name. Amen.

The Outstretched Hand

"According to your faith will it be done to you;"
and their sight was restored.
Matthew 9:29-30

When trust is perfect and there is no doubt, prayer is simply the outstretched hand ready to receive. Trust perfected is prayer perfected. Trust looks to receive the thing asked for and gets it. Trust is not a belief that God can bless or that He will bless, but that He does bless, here and now.

Trust always operates in the present tense. Hope looks toward the future. Trust looks to the present. Hope expects. Trust possesses. Trust receives what prayer acquires. So, what prayer needs, at all times, is abiding and abundant trust.

Dear Lord, my prayers still need more abiding and abundant trust so that I can receive all the blessings from Your hand. Please guide me in my trust today. Amen.

The Simplicity of Trust

*The word is near you; it is
in your mouth and in your heart.*
Romans 10:8

When people came to Him, our Lord put their trust in Him and the divinity of His mission in the forefront. He did not give a definition of trust. He knew that men would see what faith was by what faith did. They would see from its free exercise that trust grew, automatically, in His presence.

It was the product of His work, His power, and His person. Trust is too simple for verbal definition. It is too sincere and spontaneous for theological terms. The very simplicity of trust is what astounds many people.

Dear Father God, I know that trust grows in Your presence. Thank You that I can know what faith is by what faith can do. Amen.

For Sacred Use

*[Cornelius] and all his family were devout
and God-fearing; he gave generously to
those in need and prayed to God regularly.*
Acts 10:2

Devotion has great religious significance. The root meaning of *devotion* is "to devote to a sacred use."

Thus, devotion, in its true sense, has to do with religious worship. It stands intimately connected with true prayer. Devotion is the particular frame of mind found in a person entirely devoted to God.

It is the spirit of reverence and godly fear. It is a state of heart that appears before God in prayer and worship.

It is unfamiliar with things like lightness of spirit and is opposed to noise and complaining.

Devotion dwells in the realm of quietness and is still before God. It is thoughtful, serious and meditative.

Almighty God, I devote myself to Your sacred use today. I come to You in quietness and stillness of heart, please speak to me today. Amen.

March 8

His Chosen Agents

Ananias came to see me. He was a devout observer of the law and highly respected by all the Jews living there.
Acts 22:12

Devotion is a part of the very spirit of true worship and is of the nature of the spirit of prayer.

Devotion belongs to the person whose thoughts and feelings are devoted to God. Such a person has a mind given up wholly to religion and possesses a strong affection for God and a passionate love for His house.

God can wonderfully use dedicated people, for they are His chosen agents in carrying forward His plans.

Dear God, I devote my feelings and thoughts to You and I give myself wholly up to Your purposes. As Your chosen agent I want to carry forward Your plans. Amen.

March 9

The Little Things of Life

Do not be anxious about anything,
but in everything, by prayer and petition,
with thanksgiving, present your requests to God.
Philippians 4:6

The possibilities of prayer are to be seen in its accomplishments in earthly matters. Prayer reaches to everything that concerns people, whether it be the body, the mind or the soul.

Prayer takes in the needs of the body, such as food and clothes, and concerns itself with business and finances – in fact everything that belongs to this life, as well as those things that have to do with the eternal interests of the soul.

The achievements of prayer are seen not only in the large things but also in the small things.

Dear Lord, I thank You for Your hand in the important earthly matters, but also for Your presence in the little things of life. Amen.

Our Health and Happiness

I pray that you may enjoy good health and that all may go well with you, even as your soul is getting along well.
3 John 2

Earthly matters are of a lower order than the spiritual, but they concern us greatly. They are the main source of our cares and worries. They have much to do with our religion. We have bodies with needs, pains, disabilities and limitations. That which concerns our bodies necessarily engages our minds. These are subjects of prayer.

Earthly matters also greatly impact our health and happiness. They form our relations. If we do not pray about worldly matters we exclude God from a large area of our lives.

Father God, it is my desire to include You in every sphere of my life. Thank You for caring about our earthly needs and pains. Amen.

March 11

Worldly Matters

"Give us today our daily bread."
Matthew 6:11

To leave business and time out of prayer is to leave religion and eternity out of it. He who does not pray about worldly matters cannot pray with confidence about spiritual matters.

He who does not put God in his struggling toil for daily bread will never put Him in his struggle for heaven. He who does not cover and supply the needs of the body by prayer will never cover and supply the needs of his soul.

Both body and soul are dependent on God, and prayer is but the crying expression of that dependence.

Almighty God, my body and my soul yearn for You. I praise Your name for supplying my earthly and my spiritual needs. Amen.

God Cares

Cast all your anxiety on Him because He cares for you.
1 Peter 5:7

Prayer enables us to carry all our worries to God in prayer and if we doubt when we pray we upset our hearts unnecessarily.

How much needless care would we save ourselves if we just believed in prayer as the means of relieving those cares, and would learn the happy art of casting all our cares in prayer upon God, who cares for us!

Disbelief that God is concerned about even the smallest affairs that affect our happiness and comfort limits the Holy One of Israel and makes our lives altogether devoid of real happiness.

Dear God, I cast all my anxieties on You today, for You care about the smallest affairs of my life. Thank You for loving me. Amen.

An Absent Heart

"These people come near to Me with their mouth and honor
Me with their lips, but their hearts are far from Me."
Isaiah 29:13

Devotion engages the heart in prayer. It is not an easy task for the lips to try to pray while the heart is absent from it. The very essence of prayer is the spirit of devotion.

Without devotion, prayer is empty, a vain round of words. Sad to say, much of this kind of prayer prevails in the church today. This is a busy age, bustling and active, and this bustling spirit has invaded the church of God. Its religious performances are many.

True worship finds congeniality in the heart and spirit of devotion.

Lord, I want to engage all of me when I come to You in prayer. Please give me a heart and spirit of devotion so that I can truly worship You. Amen.

The Machinery of Religion

So what shall I do? I will pray with my spirit,
but I will also pray with my mind; I will sing
with my spirit, but I will also sing with my mind.
1 Corinthians 14:15

The church works at religion with the order, precision, and force of real machinery. But too often it works with the heartlessness of the machine. We pray without sincerity and we sing without true joy in our hearts.

We have music without the praise of God being in it or near it. We go to church by habit and come home all too gladly when the benediction is pronounced. We say our prayers by rote, and we are not sorry when the *Amen* is uttered.

Devote your whole heart to God and His church, and see the results of machinery inspired by Christ.

God, I don't want to work for You with the heartlessness of machinery. Please inspire my heart in all that I do for Your glory. Amen.

Your Whole Heart

Do not conform any longer to the pattern of this world,
but be transformed by the renewing of your mind.
Then you will be able to test and approve what
God's will is – His good, pleasing and perfect will.
Romans 12:2

Religion involves everything, except sometimes our hearts are not in it. It engages our hands and feet, it takes hold of our voices, it lays its hands on our money, it affects even the postures of our bodies. But it does not take hold of our affections, our desires, and cause us to worship in the presence of God.

Church membership can sometimes become a facade of respectable behavior that does not involve our hearts. Then it remains cold and unimpressed among all this outward performance, while we congratulate ourselves that we are doing wonderfully well religiously. Put your whole heart into your religion today, not just appearance!

March 16

Dear Father, please renew my heart and mind so that I may know Your good, pleasing and perfect will for my life. Amen.

To Handle Things Sacredly

For in Him we live and move and have our being.
As some of your own poets have said, "We are His offspring."
Acts 17:28

Religion sometimes lacks the spirit of devotion. We hear sermons in the same spirit with which we listen to a lecture or hear a speech. We visit the house of God just as if it were a common place; like the theater or lecture hall.

We look upon the pastor of God not as the divinely called man of God, but merely as a sort of public speaker. We handle sacred things as if they were the things of the world.

Oh, how a spirit of genuine devotion would radically change all this for the better!

Almighty God, I pray that You will open my heart for Your voice and give me a spirit of devotion for Your sacred work on earth. Amen.

Common Things Sacred

*So whether you eat or drink or whatever
you do, do it all for the glory of God.*
1 Corinthians 10:31

We need the spirit of devotion, not only to be the salt in our worldly activities, but to make our prayers real prayers. We need to put the spirit of devotion into Monday's business as well as in Sunday's worship.

We need the spirit of devotion to always recollect the presence of God and direct all things to His glory. The spirit of devotion puts God in all things.

It puts God not just in our praying and church-going, but in all the aspects of life. The spirit of devotion makes the common things of earth sacred, and the little things great.

Dear Lord, I want to do everything for Your glory. I need a spirit of devotion to make my prayers real. Please guide me. Amen.

A Sabbath on Saturday

In the same way, faith by itself, if it
is not accompanied by action, is dead.
James 2:17

With a spirit of devotion to do all things for God's glory, we go to the workplace on Monday. Directed and inspired by the very same influence we went to church with on Sunday. The spirit of devotion makes a Sabbath out of Saturday and transforms the shop or the office into a temple of God.

The spirit of devotion removes religion from being a thin veneer and puts it into our souls. With devotion in our soul, religion stops merely doing a work and becomes a heart, beating with the pulsations of vigorous and radiant life.

Dear Lord God, through a spirit of devotion I can bring glory to Your name. Please grant me a heart beating with vigor for You. Amen.

The Aroma of Religion

Dear friends, now we are children of God,
and what we will be has not yet been made known.
But we know that when He appears,
we shall be like Him, for we shall see Him as He is.
1 John 3:2

The spirit of devotion is not merely the aroma of religion, but the stalk and stem on which religion grows. It dispels idleness, and makes worship a serious and deep-rooted service that fills body, soul and spirit with a heavenly infusion.

Let us ask in all honesty: Has this highest angel of heaven, this heavenly spirit of devotion, this brightest and best angel of earth, left us? When the angel of devotion has gone, the angel of prayer has lost its wings, and it becomes a deformed and loveless thing. Never let the stalk and stem of your religion die. Water your spirit of devotion daily.

God, I pray for the heavenly spirit of devotion to return to my life so that I may worship You with new spiritual fervor. Amen.

Devotion Reacts to Prayer

Let everything that has breath
praise the LORD. Praise the LORD.
Psalm 150:6

Prayer promotes the spirit of devotion while devotion is an important aspect of effective prayer. It is easy to pray when you are in a spirit of devotion. God dwells where the spirit of devotion resides. Indeed, these graces grow nowhere else but here.

The absence of a devoted spirit means death to the graces born in a renewed heart. True worship finds kindness in the atmosphere of a spirit of devotion. While prayer is helpful to devotion, at the same time devotion reacts to prayer and helps us to pray.

Dear Father, where my spirit of devotion is there You are also. Thank You, Lord. Amen.

The Passion of Devotion

Day and night they never stop saying:
"Holy, holy, holy is the Lord God Almighty,
who was, and is, and is to come."
Revelation 4:8

The passion of devotion lies in prayer. The spirit of devotion fills the hearts of God's children and characterizes their worship. The inspiration and center of their joyful devotion is the holiness of God. That holiness of God claims their attention and inflames their devotion.

There is nothing cold, nothing dull, nothing lifeless about them or their heavenly worship. What zeal! The ministry of prayer, if it be anything worthy of the name, is a ministry of passion, a ministry of intense longing after God and His holiness.

Father God, I long to be in Your presence, singing praises with a spirit of passion and devotion to You. Amen.

Prayer Must Be Aflame

*Then I saw a new heaven and a new earth, for the
first heaven and the first earth had passed away.
And I heard a loud voice from the throne saying,
"Now the dwelling of God is with men, and He will
live with them. They will be His people, and
God Himself will be with them and be their God."*
Revelation 21:1, 3

There are no creatures without devotion in heaven.
God is there, and His very presence results in a
spirit of reverence. If we would join them in heaven
after death, we must first learn the spirit of devotion
on earth before we get there.

These living creatures are the perfect examples
and illustrations of true prayer. Prayer must be
aflame. Prayer without fervor is like a sun without
light or heat. Only he who glows for God can truly
pray.

Almighty God, please set my soul aflame with fervor for You so that I may shine brightly for all the world to see. Amen.

March 23

Actions without Devotion

My God will meet all your needs
according to His glorious riches in Christ Jesus.
Philippians 4:19

Work is not zeal. Moving about is not devotion. Activity is often the unrecognized symptom of spiritual weakness. It may be hurtful to piety when actions are made the substitute for real devotion in worship.

The child is more active than the father, who may be bearing the rule and burdens of an empire on his heart and shoulders. Enthusiasm is more active than faith, though it cannot call into action any of the omnipotent forces that faith can command.

If your spiritual life is real, a deep-toned activity will spring from it. It is an activity springing from strength and not from weakness.

Father, I don't want my actions to be without devotion and zeal. I want my spiritual life to be real so that my activities will glorify You. Amen.

The Flower and Fruit of a Holy Life

His divine power has given us everything we need for life and godliness through our knowledge of Him who called us by His own glory and goodness.
2 Peter 1:3

In the nature of things, religion must show much of its growth above ground. The flower and fruit of a holy life, abounding in good works, must be seen. It cannot be otherwise. But the surface growth must be based on a vigorous growth of unseen life and hidden roots.

The roots of religion must go down deep in the renewed nature to be seen on the outside. There should be much of the invisible and the underground growth, or else the life will be feeble and short-lived, and the external growth fruitless.

Lord, I want to bear the fruit of Your Spirit in my life. Please make my roots grow ever deeper. Amen.

Too Busy with God's Work

Those who hope in the LORD will renew their strength.
They will soar on wings like eagles; they will run
and not grow weary, they will walk and not be faint.
Isaiah 40:31

To run and not grow weary is the beginning of the whole matter of activity and strength. All this is the result of waiting on God.

There may be lots of activities created by enthusiasm. Activity often continues at the expense of more solid, useful elements and generally to the total neglect of prayer. To be too busy with God's work to commune with Him, to be busy with doing church work without taking time to talk to God about His work, is the highway to backsliding.

In spite of great activity, the work will be helpless without the cultivation and the maturity of the graces of prayer.

Father God, please help me not to become so busy with Your work that I don't take time to consult with You about what You want me to do. Amen.

A Life with Feeling

*"Therefore I tell you, whatever
you ask for in prayer, believe that you
have received it, and it will be yours."*
Mark 11:24

Trust, like life, is feeling. An unfelt life is a contradiction. Trust is the most felt of all qualities. It is *all* feeling, and it only works by love. An unfelt love is as impossible as an unfelt trust. The trust we are speaking about is a conviction. Trust sees God doing things here and now.

It transforms hope into the reality of fulfillment and changes promise into present possession. We know when we trust, just as we know when we see. Trust sees, receives, holds. Trust is its own witness.

Dear God, thank You that our trust in You transforms our hope into fulfilled realities. You are a wonderful God. Amen.

March 27

The Golden Rule – Prayer

He has showed you, O man, what is good.
To act justly and to love mercy
and to walk humbly with your God.
Micah 6:8

The ministry of prayer has been the special distinction of all God's saints. The energy and the soul of their work have come from their prayer lives.

Because the need for help outside of man is so great – given man's natural inability to always judge kindly, justly, and truly and to act out the Golden Rule – prayer is instructed by Christ to enable man to act in all these things according to His divine will.

By prayer, the ability is secured to feel the law of love, to speak according to the law of love, and to do everything in harmony with God's law of love.

Lord God, You gave prayer to us so that through Christ we are able to do all things for Your glory. I want to walk in harmony with Your law of love. Amen.

March 28

A Current of Prayer

*We will give our attention to prayer
and the ministry of the word.*
Acts 6:4

Prayer must be incessant and should not lack desire, spirit or action. The knees may not always be bent, but the spirit is always in the act and communication of prayer.

The spirit of prayer should sweetly rule and adjust all times and occasions. Our activities and work should be performed in the same spirit that makes our devotion and our prayer time sacred.

Blessed is the person of God who thus understands prayer, at any point, at any time. A full current of prayer is seen flowing from him.

Dear Father, I want my spirit to always be bent to You in prayer, even when I'm not on my knees. Amen.

Trust from the Heart

Trust in the LORD.
Psalm 37:3

The trust in history or records may be a passive thing, but trust in a person, strengthens the quality. The trust that supplies prayer centers in a Person.

Trust goes even further than this. The trust that inspires our prayer must not only be in the Person of God, and of Christ, but in their ability and willingness to grant the things we pray for. And to trust that, as our Lord taught, a condition of effective prayer is not from the head but from the heart.

The strong promise of our Lord brings faith down to the present and counts on a present answer.

Dear Lord, I believe that by trusting in You, You will grant us the desires of our hearts. I praise Your name. Amen.

Our Great High Priest

He offered up prayers and
petitions with loud cries and tears.
Hebrews 5:7

Christ Jesus, our Great High Priest, was a gracious Comforter, and an all-powerful Intercessor. The Holy Spirit enters into all our blessed relations of fellowship and authority, and helps with all the tenderness, fullness and efficiency of Christ.

Was Christ the Christ of prayer? Did He seek the silence, the solitude, and the darkness so that He could pray? Does He sit at the right hand of God in heaven to pray for us there? Of course!

Then how truly does the great Comforter, the Holy Spirit, represent Jesus Christ as the Christ of prayer!

Almighty God, I want to thank You for giving us a great High Priest, a gracious Comforter and an all-powerful Intercessor. Amen.

March 31

April

Prayer and Desire

The prayer of a righteous man is powerful and effective.
James 5:16

To desire something is not merely a simple wish. In the realm of spiritual affairs, it is so important that one could almost say desire is an absolute essential of prayer. Desire precedes and accompanies prayer. Prayer is the verbal expression of desire. Prayer comes out into the open. Desire is silent. Prayer is heard. The deeper the desire, the stronger the prayer.

Without desire, prayer is a meaningless mumble of words. Such uninterested, formal praying, with no heart, feeling, or real desire, is to be avoided like a plague. Its exercise is a waste of precious time, and no real blessing results from it.

Dear God, all that I desire is to worship You. Please guide me that my prayers will be accompanied by a strong desire to do Your will. Amen.

Where Grace Abounds, Song Abounds

May the peoples praise You, O God.
Psalm 67:5

When God is in a person's heart, heaven is present and melody is found there. This is as true in the private life of the believer as it is in the congregations of the saints. The decay of singing means the decline of grace in the heart and the absence of God's presence from the people.

The main purpose of singing is for God's ear; to attract His attention and to please Him. Certainly it is not for the glorification of the paid choir, nor to draw people to the church, but it is for the glory of God and the good of the souls of the congregation.

Father God, I want to sing praises to Your name. I want to glorify and please You with my song, for You have been good to me. Amen.

Love Grows as Gratitude Grows

Because He turned His ear to me,
I will call on Him as long as I live.
Psalm 116:2

Love is the child of gratitude. Love grows as gratitude is felt and then breaks out into praise and thanksgiving to God. Answered prayers cause gratitude, and gratitude brings forth a love that declares to never stop praying. Gratitude and love move to larger and increased prayer.

Consideration of God's mercies not only creates gratitude, but leads to a large consecration to God of all that we have and are. Thus, prayer, thanksgiving, and consecration are all inseparably linked together.

Dear Lord God, I praise You because I have been fearfully and wonderfully made. Thank You for loving me. Amen.

April 3

Heavenly Appetites

*"Blessed are those who hunger and thirst
for righteousness, for they will be filled."*
Matthew 5:6

Heaven-given appetites are proof of a renewed heart and the evidence of a stirring spiritual life. Spiritual desires belong to a soul made alive to God. As the renewed soul hungers and thirsts after righteousness, these holy desires break out into prayer.

In prayer we are dependent on the name and power of Jesus Christ to satisfy our hunger for Him. The vital basis of prayer is seated in the human heart. It is not simply our need; it is the heart's desire for what we need and for what we feel urged to pray about. Desire is the will in action.

Father, my soul thirsts and hungers after You. Thank You for satisfying my every need. Amen.

Burning Desire

You say, "I am rich; I have acquired wealth and do not need a thing." But you do not realize that you are wretched, pitiful, poor, blind and naked.
Revelation 3:17

It is impossible to ask whether the feebleness of our desire for God is the cause of our lack of prayer. Do we really feel this inward hunger for heavenly treasures? No, the fire burns entirely too low. This, we should remember, was the major cause of the sad condition of the Laodicean Christians.

Our hearts need to be renewed, not only to get the evil out of them, but to get the good into them too. They need to be renewed so that the inspiration to turn toward heavenly things is a strong, moving desire.

Dear God, sometimes my feeble desire is the reason for my lack of prayer. Please create in me a pure heart and renew the right spirit within me. Amen.

Invisible Gratitude Becomes Visible Thanksgiving

One of them, when he saw he was healed, came back, praising God in a loud voice. He threw himself at Jesus' feet and thanked Him – and he was a Samaritan.
Luke 17:15-16

Thanksgiving is verbal, positive and active. It is the giving out of something to God. Thanksgiving is done in the open. Gratitude is secret, silent, passive, not showing its being until expressed in praise and thanksgiving.

Gratitude is felt in the heart. Thanksgiving is the expression of that inward feeling. Thanksgiving is just what the word itself signifies – the giving of thanks to God. It is giving something to God in words that we feel in our heart for blessings received.

Dear Father, I am grateful to You for so many blessings received from Your hand. My heart is filled with gratitude toward You. I praise Your name. Amen.

A Fiery Church

Never be lacking in zeal, but keep your spiritual fervor.
Romans 12:11

God Himself is all fire; and His church, if it is to be like Him, must also be like white heat. God expects to be represented by a fiery church. The only things that His church can afford to be on fire about are the great, eternal interests of God-given faith.

Our Lord was the incarnate opposite of intolerant and noisy speech. Yet the zeal of God's house consumed Him. And the world is still feeling the glow of His consuming flame. They are responding to it with an ever-increasing readiness and an even larger response.

God, I want to be part of a church on fire for You. Help me to never be lacking in zeal but glowing with passion for You. Amen.

Zest for Life

"You are neither cold nor hot. I wish you were either one or the other! So, because you are lukewarm – neither hot nor cold – I am about to spit you out of My mouth."
Revelation 3:15-16

Two things are intolerable to God – insincerity and lukewarmness. Lack of heart and heat are two things God hates. He said that to the Laodiceans.

True prayer must be aflame. The Christian life and character need to be on fire. If man is not wholly interested in the things of heaven, he is not interested in them at all. The fiery souls are those who conquer in the day of battle.

The stronghold of God is taken only by those who storm it in worshipful earnestness and besiege it with fiery, unshaken zeal.

Lord, I know that You hate lukewarmness. I want to be wholly interested in the things of heaven. Please help and guide me through Your Holy Spirit. Amen.

April 8

Passion for Christ

"Zeal for Your house will consume me."
John 2:17

Love is kindled in a flame, and zeal is its fuel. Flame is the air that true Christian experience breathes. It feeds on fire. It can withstand anything except a weak flame.

A lack of passion in prayer is a sure sign of the lack of depth and intensity of desire. To reduce fervor is to retire from God. He can and will pardon sin when the repentant one prays. Fire is the motivating power in prayer.

Religious principles that do not come out of fire have neither force nor effect. Passion is the soul of prayer.

Dear God, I don't want to be lacking in spiritual fervor. Ignite the flames of passion in my soul so that I may serve You wholeheartedly. Amen.

No Prayer without Flame

*May my prayer be set before You like incense; may
the lifting up of my hands be like the evening sacrifice.*
Psalm 141:2

The early Methodists had no heating in their churches. They said that the flame in the pew and the fire in the pulpit must be sufficient to keep them warm. And we, today, need to have the live coal from God's altar in our hearts.

This flame is not mental power or fleshly energy. It is the very being of the Spirit of God. Prayer ascends by fire. Flame gives prayer access as well as wings. It gives prayer acceptance as well as energy. There is no incense without fire, no prayer without flame.

Father God, I want the burning coal from Your altar in my heart. I pray, Lord, for You to ignite my heart through the power of Your Spirit. Amen.

Babbling or Prayer?

My soul thirsts for God, for the living God.
Psalm 42:2

Prayer is not the rehearsal of a mere performance. It is not an indefinite, widespread demand. Prayer is a necessary phase of spiritual habit, but it ceases to be prayer when it is done by habit alone.

It is the depth and strength of spiritual desire that gives intensity to prayer. Many things may be listed and much ground covered. Does desire map out the region to be covered? The answer depends on whether our petitioning is babbling or prayer.

The urgency of our desire holds us to the thing desired with sustained courage. It stays, pleads, persists and refuses to let go until the blessing has been given.

Lord, please guide me so that my prayers will never be mere babbling, but earnest, heartfelt prayer. Amen.

April 11

Basis of Prayer

*"Blessed are those who hunger and thirst
for righteousness, for they will be filled."*
Matthew 5:6

Desire shoots at its objective. There may be many things that are desired, but they are specifically and individually felt and expressed. It is this singleness of desire, this definite yearning, that counts in prayer and drives it directly to the center of supply.

This is the basis of prayer that expects an answer. It is that strong, inward desire that has entered the spiritual appetite and demands to be satisfied.

For us, it is entirely true and frequent that our prayers operate in the dry area of a mere wish or in the lifeless area of a memorized prayer.

Pray fervently and with a sincere yearning for the Lord, and He will draw near to you and satisfy your needs.

Dear God, thank You that we may know that those who hunger and thirst for You, will be satisfied. Amen.

A New Discovery

I will not let you go, unless you bless me.
Genesis 32:26

Sometimes our prayers are merely stereotyped expressions of set phrases. The freshness and life has gone out long ago.

Without desire, there is no burden of the soul, no vision, and no glow of faith. There is no strong pressure, no holding on to God with a despairing grasp.

God draws very close to the praying soul. To see God, know God, and live for God – these form the objective of all true prayer. So, to those who pray like this, the Bible becomes a new discovery, and Christ a new Savior by the light and revelation gained through your prayers.

Dear Father, through prayer we can discover and experience You anew each day. Thank You for drawing close to the praying soul. Amen.

Discerning our Desires

One thing I ask of the LORD, this is what I seek:
that I may dwell in the house of the LORD
all the days of my life, to gaze upon the beauty
of the LORD and to seek Him in His temple.
Psalm 27:4

Desire is the will in action. It is a strong, conscious longing that is energized in the inner man for some great good. It contains choice, attitude, and fire. Prayer, based on these characteristics, is genuine and specific.

Holy desire is helped by devout study. Meditation on our spiritual needs and God's ability to satisfy them, helps desire to grow. Serious thought, practiced before praying, increases desire. It makes prayer more insistent and tends to save us from the danger of wandering thoughts.

God, please guide me through Your Holy Spirit as I meditate on Your Word. You are worthy of our praise. Amen.

Closely Related

Devote yourselves to prayer,
being watchful and thankful.
Colossians 4:2

Prayer, praise and thanksgiving all go together. A close relationship exists among them. The Scriptures join these three things together.

Psalms is filled with many songs of praise and hymns of thanksgiving, all pointing back to the results of prayer.

Thanksgiving includes gratitude. In fact, thanksgiving is the expression of an inward, conscious gratitude to God for mercies received.

Gratitude is an inward emotion of the soul, involuntarily arising therein, while thanksgiving is the voluntary expression of gratitude.

Dear Father God, I want to give thanks to You with a grateful heart because You have been good to me. Your love endures forever. Amen.

April 15

Gratitude

*The Lord has done great things
for us, and we are filled with joy.*
Psalm 126:3

Gratitude arises from a contemplation of the goodness of God. It arises when we meditate on what God has done for us. Gratitude and thanksgiving both point to, and have to do with God and His mercies. The heart is consciously grateful to God. The soul gives expression to that heartfelt gratitude to God in words or acts.

Gratitude is born of meditation on God's grace and mercy. Praise is brought about by gratitude and a conscious obligation to God for mercies given. As we think of mercies past, our hearts are inwardly moved to gratitude.

Dear God, my heart is filled with gratitude toward You for all the grace and mercy You have for Your children. Amen.

Pray for Desire

What is more, I consider everything a loss compared
to the surpassing greatness of knowing Christ
Jesus my Lord, for whose sake I have lost all things.
I consider them rubbish, that I may gain Christ.
Philippians 3:8

Our judgment tells us that we ought to pray, even if we discover that desire is absent. In such circumstances, we ought to pray for the desire to pray. This desire is God-given and heaven-born.

When desire has been given, we should pray according to its principles. The lack of spiritual desire should grieve us and lead us to mourn its absence. We should earnestly seek for its prize so that our praying can be an expression of the soul's sincere desire.

Almighty God, I pray that You will increase and inspire my desire to pray. I want my prayers to be powerful and effective. Amen.

Prayer Looks to the Future

Be joyful always; pray continually;
give thanks in all circumstances,
for this is God's will for you in Christ Jesus.
1 Thessalonians 5:16-18

Gratitude and thanksgiving always look back at the past, although they also take in the present. But prayer always looks to the future. Thanksgiving deals with things already received. Prayer deals with things desired, asked for, and expected.

Prayer turns to gratitude and praise when the things asked for have been granted by God. As prayer brings things to us that produce gratitude and thanksgiving, so praise and gratitude promote prayer and encourage more and better praying.

Father, Your will for us is to pray continually and give thanks in all circumstances. Please help me do this through Your Holy Spirit. Amen.

Gratitude and Murmuring

And be thankful ... as you teach and
admonish one another with all wisdom,
and as you sing psalms, hymns and spiritual
songs with gratitude in your hearts to God.
Colossians 3:15-16

Gratitude and thanksgiving to God stand opposed to our murmuring and complaints about our situation. Gratitude and murmuring never abide in the same heart at the same time. An unappreciative spirit has no standing beside gratitude and praise.

True prayer banishes complaining and promotes gratitude and thanksgiving. Dissatisfaction at one's lot, and a disposition to be discontented with things that come to us in the providence of God, are foes to gratitude and enemies to thanksgiving.

Lord God, I don't want dissatisfaction to stand in the way of being grateful and giving thanks to You. Please grant me an appreciative and content spirit. Amen.

April 19

A Consecrated Life = Prayer + Thanksgiving

With thanksgiving, present your requests to God.
Philippians 4:6

Wherever there is true prayer, thanksgiving and gratitude are ready to respond to its fulfillment when it comes. As prayer brings the answer, so the answer brings forth gratitude and praise.

As prayer sets God to work, so answered prayer sets thanksgiving to work. Thanksgiving follows answered prayer just as day succeeds night.

True prayer and gratitude lead to full consecration, and consecration leads to more and better praying. A consecrated life is a life of both prayer and thanksgiving.

Dear God, I want to live a consecrated life of prayer and thanksgiving before You. Guide me through the power of Your Spirit. Amen.

Sing Praises!

"He who sacrifices thank offerings honors Me,
and he prepares the way so that I
may show him the salvation of God."
Psalm 50:23

Praise is definitely committed to prayer. Praise is dependent on prayer for its full volume and its sweet melody. Singing is the usual method of praise. The singing service in our churches is important, for according to the character of our singing, the genuineness of our praises will be measured.

The singing may be directed in such a way as to have in it elements that deprave and debauch prayer. It may be so directed as to drive away things like thanksgiving and praise.

Most of the singing in our churches today is entirely foreign to hearty, sincere praise to God.

Praise God with your sincere songs of joy today and every day.

Lord, I want to sing songs of praise and joy to You. Please help me so that my singing to You may be sincere. Amen.

April 21

The Fragrance of Prayer

Through Jesus, therefore, let us continually offer to God
a sacrifice of praise – the fruit of lips that confess His name.
Hebrews 13:15

The spirit of prayer and of true praise go hand in hand. Both are often entirely driven away by the thoughtless singing in our congregations. A lot of the singing lacks serious thought and is devoid of a devotional spirit.

Giving thanks is the very life of prayer. It is its fragrance and music, its poetry and its crown. Prayer, bringing the desired answer, breaks out into praise and thanksgiving. Whatever interferes with and injures the spirit of prayer necessarily hurts and dissipates the spirit of praise.

Father God, my offer to You is my sacrifice of praise. I want to sing of Your love and goodness forever. Amen.

Spiritual Singing

*Let everything that has breath praise
the LORD. Praise the LORD.*
Psalm 150:6

The heart must have in it the grace of prayer to sing
the praises of God. Spiritual singing is not done by
musical taste or talent, but by the grace of God in
your heart. Nothing helps praise so mightily as a
gracious revival of true religion in the church.

The conscious presence of God inspires song.
The angels and the glorified ones in heaven do not
need choirs to chime in with their heavenly praise
and worship.

They are not dependent on singing schools to
teach them the notes and scale of singing. Their
singing involuntarily breaks forth from the heart.

*Thank You, Lord God, for inspiring our songs and
prayers through Your presence. Amen.*

God's Presence Results in Singing

*How good it is to sing praises to our God,
how pleasant and fitting to praise Him.*
Psalm 147:1

God is always present in the heavenly assemblies of the angels. His glorious presence creates the song, teaches the singing, and infuses the notes of praise.

The presence of God results in singing and thanksgiving, while the absence of God from our congregations is the death of song, and makes the singing lifeless, cold, and formal.

God's conscious presence in our churches would bring back the days of praise and would restore the full chorus of song.

Lord, together with the psalmist I say, "How good it is to sing praises to our God, how pleasant and fitting to praise Him." Amen.

A Spiritual Desire

Like newborn babies, crave pure spiritual
milk, so that by it you may grow up.
1 Peter 2:2

A sense of need creates earnest desire. Hunger is an active sense of physical need. It prompts the request for food. In the same way, the inward awareness of spiritual need creates desire, and desire creates prayer.

Desire is a longing in our hearts for something that we do not have. Spiritual desire is the evidence of new life in Christ.

It is born in the renewed soul: The absence of this holy desire in the heart is proof that there has been a decline in spiritual joy or that the new birth has never taken place.

God, I pray that my spiritual joy would not decline. I pray for my soul to be renewed by You every day for Your glory. Amen.

April 25

Specific Prayers

Is any one of you in trouble? He should pray.
Is anyone happy? Let him sing songs of praise.
James 5:13

God does so much for us, but to get all the things we need, we need to pray a certain kind of prayer. We need to be specific and particular and bring to God, through prayer and thanksgiving, our particular requests; the things we greatly desire. And with it all, accompanying all these requests, there must be thanksgiving.

It is wonderful to know that what God wants us to do on earth, we will be engaged in doing for eternity.

Praise and thanksgiving will be our blessed employment while we remain in heaven. Nor will we ever grow weary of this pleasing task.

God Almighty, I present my requests to You by prayer and petition, with thanksgiving. Thank You for hearing my prayers. Amen.

April 26

A Praising Spirit

Praise awaits You, O God, in Zion;
to You our vows will be fulfilled.
Psalm 65:1

The spirit of praise was once the boast of the early church. This spirit rested on the tabernacles of the early Christians, as a cloud of glory out of which God shone and spoke. It filled their temples with the perfume of costly, flaming incense.

That this spirit of praise is sadly deficient in our present-day congregations must be evident to every careful observer. That it is a mighty force in projecting the gospel, must be equally evident.

To restore the spirit of praise to our congregations should be one of the main objectives of every Christian.

Lord, I want the spirit of praise to return to our congregations so that Your name will be glorified over all the earth. Amen.

April 27

Waiting for the Spirit

All of them were filled with the Holy Spirit.
Acts 2:4

The promise of the Holy Spirit to the disciples was realized only after many days of persistent prayer. The promise was clear and definite that the disciples should be gifted with power from on high; they had to stay in Jerusalem.

The fulfillment of the promise depended on the waiting. And it is significant that it was while they were praying, resting their expectations on the surety of the promise, that the Holy Spirit fell upon them and they were all filled. The promise and the prayer went hand in hand.

Thank You, Lord, that You fill us with Your Holy Spirit if we rest our expectations on Your promises while we pray and wait on You. Amen.

The Famous Day of Pentecost

On one occasion, while He was eating with them,
He gave them this command: "Do not leave
Jerusalem, but wait for the gift My Father promised,
which you have heard Me speak about."
Acts 1:4

After Jesus Christ made this promise to His disciples, He ascended to heaven. Yet the promise given by Him of sending the Holy Spirit was not fulfilled only by His enthronement.

The answer is found in the fact that His disciples, with the women, spent several days in that Upper Room, in continued prayer. It was prayer that brought to pass the famous Day of Pentecost. And as it was then, so it can be today.

Prayer can bring a Pentecost today if there is the same kind of praying, for the promise has not lost its power and vitality.

God, I know that persistent, heartfelt prayer can achieve great things in this world. Please keep me on my knees. Amen.

April 29

The Abundant Pardon

"Jesus, Son of David, have mercy on me."
Mark 10:47

The promises of God to all kinds of sinners are the same. God's promises are fulfilled when sinners repent and ask God for forgiveness.

The praying sinner receives mercy because his prayer is grounded on the promise that if we confess our sins, God will forgive us and purify us. The remorseful one who seeks after God obtains mercy because there is a definite promise of mercy to all who seek the Lord's face.

Prayer always brings forgiveness to the seeking soul. The abundant pardon is dependent upon the promise made real by God's promise to the sinner.

Lord, thank You for Your promise that if we confess our sins, You are faithful and just and will forgive us our sins and purify us from all unrighteousness. Amen.

May

Prayer ... without Heart?

*Never be lacking in zeal, but keep your
spiritual fervor, serving the Lord.*
Romans 12:11

Prayer, without burning enthusiasm does not help
your situation, because it has nothing to give.

Prayer without enthusiasm has no heart. Heart,
soul and mind must find a place in real praying.
Heaven must be moved to feel the force of this crying unto God.

Paul was a notable example of a man with a fervent spirit of prayer. His petitioning was all-con-
suming. It centered immovably upon the object of
his desire and the God who was able to meet it.

*Dear God, I want to have the fervent spirit of Paul.
Please guide me in Your truth today. Amen.*

May 1

School of Trouble

Who shall separate us from the love of Christ?
Shall trouble or hardship or persecution or
famine or nakedness or danger or sword?
Romans 8:35

What an infinite variety there is in the troubles of life! No two people have the same troubles in a certain area. God deals with no two of His children in the same way.

Just as God varies His treatment of His children, so trouble is varied. God does not repeat Himself; He does not have one pattern that He uses for everyone. He deals with every child individually, according to his or her specific situation.

Lord, troubles come in various shapes and sizes.
Thank You for treating each of Your children in a unique
and special way. Amen.

Feeble Prayer

*Then Jesus told His disciples a parable to show them
that they should always pray and not give up.*
Luke 18:1

Our Lord warns us against feeble prayer. This means that we must possess enough enthusiasm to carry us through the severe and long periods of pleading prayer. Fire makes one alert, vigilant, and brings one out as more than a conqueror.

The atmosphere about us is too heavily charged with resisting forces for lifeless prayers to make any progress. It takes heat, fervency and fire to push through to the heavens where God dwells with His saints.

Fervency before God counts in the hour of prayer and finds a speedy and rich reward at God's hands.

*Dear Father, please grant me heat, fervency and fire
to push through my troubles and toward You in heaven.
Amen.*

May 3

Trouble Has No Power

*"He causes His sun to rise on the evil and the good,
and sends rain on the righteous and the unrighteous."*
Matthew 5:45

As trouble is not sinful in itself, neither is it the evidence of sin. Good and bad alike experience trouble. Trouble is no evidence whatsoever of divine displeasure. Numerous Scripture verses contradict such an idea.

Job is an example of where God bore explicit testimony to his deep piety, and yet permitted Satan to afflict Job beyond any other man for wise and beneficial purposes. Trouble has no power in itself to interfere with the relationship of a saint to God.

Dear God, I know that trouble has no power to interfere with my relationship with You. For that, I thank You. Amen.

May 4

A Fervent Spirit

As the deer pants for streams of water, so my soul pants
for You, O God. My soul thirsts for God, for
the living God. When can I go and meet with God?
Psalm 42:1-2

Fervency has its seat in the heart, not in the brain or intellect of the mind. Fervency is the pulse and movement of the emotional nature.

It is not our job to create fervency of spirit at our own command, but we can ask God to plant it in our hearts. Then, it is ours to nourish and cherish.

The process of personal salvation is not just to pray and express our desires to God, but to acquire a fervent spirit and seek to cultivate it.

Ask God to create a spirit of fervent prayer in you and keep it alive.

Father, I pray that You will plant in me fervency of spirit. I also ask You to help and guide me in nourishing and cherishing this fervency of heart. Amen.

May 5

When Trouble Comes

*"Come to Me, all you who are weary
and burdened, and I will give you rest."*
Matthew 11:28

The most natural thing to do is to carry your troubles to the Lord and seek grace, patience and submission there. How natural and reasonable for the oppressed, broken, bruised soul to bow low and seek the face of God!

Unfortunately, trouble does not always drive people to God in prayer. It is sad when a person does not know how to pray when troubles discourage him. Blessed is the man who is driven by trouble to his knees in prayer!

Almighty God, I carry all my worries and burdens to You. I know that You will comfort me and give me rest. Thank You. Amen.

The Objective of Desire

The eyes of the LORD range throughout the earth
to strengthen those whose hearts are
fully committed to Him. You have done
a foolish thing, and from now on you will be at war.
2 Chronicles 16:9

Fervency, just like prayer, has to do with God. Desire always has an objective. If we desire at all, we desire *something*. The degree of enthusiasm with which we form our spiritual desires will always serve to determine the earnestness of our praying.

Prayer must be clothed with fervency, strength, and power. It is the force that, centered on God, determines the amount of Himself given out for earthly good.

People who are fervent in spirit are bent on attaining righteousness, and all the other characteristics that God desires His children to have.

Dear God, clothe me with fervency, strength and power through Your indwelling Spirit. In Jesus' name I pray. Amen.

May 7

Trouble and Prayer

*No temptation has seized you
except what is common to man.*
1 Corinthians 10:13

Trouble and prayer are closely related to each other. Prayer is of great value to trouble. Trouble often drives people to God in prayer, while prayer is but the voice of people in trouble. There is great value in prayer in times of trouble.

Prayer often delivers one from trouble and, more often, gives strength to bear trouble, ministers comfort in trouble, and creates patience in the midst of trouble.

Wise is the person who knows his True Source of strength and who doesn't fail to pray in times of trouble.

Thank You, God, for delivering me in times of trouble. I know that there is power and great value in prayer. I praise Your name. Amen.

Not Just Sunshine and Pleasure

*Man born of woman
is of few days and full of trouble.*
Job 14:1

Trouble is part of a person's everyday life on earth.
Trouble has the power to fill a person with unnecessary despair and stress.

The view of life that expects nothing but sunshine and looks only for pleasure and flowers, is an entirely false view and shows supreme ignorance. It is such people who are so sadly disappointed and surprised when trouble breaks into their lives.

These are the people who don't know God, who know nothing of His disciplinary dealings with His people and who are prayerless.

God, You say in Your Word that we will never be tempted beyond what we can bear. Thank You for delivering us in times of trouble when we come to You in prayer. Amen.

All My Longings ...

All my longings lie open before You,
O LORD; my sighing is not hidden from You.
Psalm 38:9

What a cheerful thought! Our groanings are not hidden from the eyes of the Lord to whom we pray.

The incentive for fervency of spirit before God is exactly the same as it is for consistent prayer. While fervency is not prayer, it flows from an earnest soul and is precious in the sight of God. Fervency in prayer is the forerunner of what God will do in answer to prayer.

When we seek His face in prayer, God has to give us the desires of our hearts in proportion to the fervency of spirit we exhibit.

Dear Father, I seek Your face as I come to You in prayer. I pray for my fervency of spirit to increase. Amen.

Trouble as God's Servant

In this you greatly rejoice, though now for a little
while you may have had to suffer grief in all kinds
of trials. These have come so that your faith
may be proved genuine and may result in praise,
glory and honor when Jesus Christ is revealed.
1 Peter 1:6-7

Trouble is under the control of God and is one of His most efficient agents in fulfilling His purposes and in perfecting His saints. God's hand is in every trouble that happens in the lives of His people.

This is not to say that He directly and randomly orders every unpleasant experience of life or that He is personally responsible for every painful and afflicting thing.

However, no trouble is ever turned loose in this world, but it comes with divine permission to do its painful work with God's hand involved, carrying out His gracious acts of redemption.

O Lord, You have searched me and You know me.
You are involved in every aspect of my life. Thank You
for being near me in times of trouble. Amen.

May 11

Red Hot Prayer

John answered them all, "I baptize you with water.
But one more powerful than I will come, the thongs
of whose sandals I am not worthy to untie.
He will baptize you with the Holy Spirit and with fire."
Luke 3:16

Prayers must be red hot. It is the fervent prayer that is effective. It takes fire to make prayers work. God wants warmhearted servants. We are to be baptized with the Holy Spirit and with fire.

Fervency is warmth of soul. If our faith does not set us on fire, it is because our hearts have become cold. God dwells in a flame; the Holy Spirit descends in fire. To be absorbed in God's will and to be so earnest about doing His will, is a symptom of a believer who prays effectively.

Dear God, You promised in Your Word that You would give us a new heart and a new spirit. I want my prayers to You to have power and bring change. Amen.

May 12

Under Divine Control

We know that in all things God works
for the good of those who love Him.
Romans 8:28

This Scripture verse is so often quoted, but the depth of its meaning is rarely fully grasped. All things are under God's divine control. Trouble is neither above nor beyond His control. It is not independent of God.

No matter from what source trouble springs or from where it arises, God is sufficiently wise and able to lay His hand upon it and work it into His plans and purposes concerning the highest welfare of His people.

Father God, I know that all things work together for the good of those who love You. Thank You for having my highest welfare in Your plans. Amen.

A Season of Trial

The Lord disciplines those He loves, and
He punishes everyone He accepts as a son.
Hebrews 12:6

Trouble belongs to the disciplinary part of the government of God. This is a life where the human race is on probation. It is a season of trial.

Trouble does not always arise to punish a person. It belongs to what the Scriptures call "chastening". Strictly speaking, punishment does not belong to this life. God wants to discipline His people. Disciplining is a corrective process in His plans concerning man.

It is because of this that prayer comes in when trouble arises. Prayer should be part of every aspect of your day-to-day life!

O Father, help me to see that disciplining from You is a corrective process in Your plans concerning me. Amen.

Temptation, Trial and Trouble

*Consider it pure joy, my brothers, whenever
you face trials of many kinds, because you know
that the testing of your faith develops perseverance.*
James 1:2-3

Three words are used in the descriptions of divine discipline: temptation, trial and trouble. Temptation is really evil arising from the Devil or born in the nature of man.

Trial is testing. It proves us, tests us, and makes us stronger when we submit to the trial and work together with God to overcome it.

The third word is trouble, which covers all the painful, grievous events of life.

It is enough to know that trouble in God's hand becomes His agent to accomplish His gracious work concerning those who recognize Him in prayer, and who work together with Him.

Thank You, God, that You use trouble in our lives to accomplish Your gracious work and that the testing of our faith develops perseverance. Amen.

May 15

Divine Providence

*For hardship does not spring from the soil,
nor does trouble sprout from the ground. Yet man
is born to trouble as surely as sparks fly upward.*
Job 5:6-7

Let us accept the idea that trouble does not arise by chance, nor does it occur by accident. Trouble naturally belongs to God's moral government and is one of His invaluable agents in governing the world.

When we realize this, we can better understand much of what is recorded in the Scriptures and can have a clearer concept of God's dealings with ancient Israel.

In God's dealings with them, we find what is called a history of Divine Providence.

Almighty God, I realize that You can use our troubles to accomplish great things in this world for Your glory. Thank You, Lord. Amen.

May 16

The Most Appropriate Thing

"Call upon Me in the day of trouble;
I will deliver you, and you will honor Me."
Psalm 50:15

There is a distinct note of comfort in John's gospel for the praying saints of the Lord. Jesus Himself said to His disciples, "I will not leave you as orphans" (John 14:18). All this has been said so that we may realize the necessity of prayer in trouble.

In times of trouble, where does prayer come in? Prayer is the most appropriate thing for a soul to do in times of trouble. Prayer recognizes God in the day of trouble.

Prayer sees God's hand in the midst of trouble and prays to Him. Blessed is he who knows how to turn to God in times of trouble.

God, when the troubles of life have left me destitute, please help me to turn to You in prayer, for You will deliver me. Amen.

Prayer Brings Comfort

*It was good for me to be afflicted
so that I might learn Your decrees.*
Psalm 119:71

Prayer in times of trouble brings comfort, help, hope and blessings that, while not making the trouble disappear, enables the saint to handle it better and to submit to the will of God.

Prayer opens the eyes to see God's hand in trouble. Prayer does not interpret God's providence, but it does justify it and recognize God in it. Prayer enables us to see wise ends in trouble. Prayer in trouble drives us away from unbelief, saves us from doubt, and delivers us from all vain and foolish questioning because of our painful experiences.

Father, please help me to pray in trouble so that I can be saved from doubt through Your mercy and grace. Amen.

May 18

All Kinds of Troubles

"Each day has enough trouble of its own."
Matthew 6:34

Some troubles only exist in the mind. Some are anticipated troubles that never come. Others are past troubles, and it is foolish to worry over them. Present troubles are the only ones requiring attention and demanding prayer.

Some troubles are self-originated; we are their authors. Some of these originate involuntarily; some arise from our ignorance; some come from our carelessness.

All this can be readily admitted without breaking the force of the statement that troubles are the subjects of prayer and should therefore drive us to prayer.

Almighty God, I pray that You will open my eyes in my times of trouble to realize that I only need to come to You in prayer. Amen.

May 19

Outside the Realm of Prayer

For our light and momentary troubles are achieving
for us an eternal glory that far outweighs them all.
2 Corinthians 4:17

Some troubles are human in their origin. They arise from secondary causes. They originate with other people, but we are the sufferers. Who has not at some time suffered at the hands of others? But even these are allowed to happen in the order of God's providence, and may be prayed over.

Why should we not carry our hurts, our wrongs, and our hardships, caused by the acts of others to God in prayer? Are such things outside the realm of prayer? Are they exceptions to the rule of prayer? Not at all.

God can and will lay His hand upon all such events in answer to prayer.

Father God, I bring all my hurts, wrongs and hardships to You in prayer. Thank You for laying Your hand upon my life to heal my suffering. Amen.

To See God in All

The LORD gave and the LORD has taken away;
may the name of the LORD be praised.
Job 1:21

When we survey all the sources from which trouble comes, we realize two invaluable truths: first, our troubles, in the end, are of the Lord. He is in all of them and is interested in us when they press and bruise us.

Secondly, in our troubles, no matter what the cause, whether of ourselves or people or devils or even God Himself, we are warranted in taking them to God in prayer and seeking to get the greatest spiritual benefits out of them.

Dear God, I want to see Your face and praise Your name even in the midst of my troubles. Please guide me through Your Holy Spirit. Amen.

May 21

Prayer Prepares the Heart

*This poor man called, and the LORD
heard him; He saved him out of all his troubles.*
Psalm 34:6

Prayer in times of trouble tends to bring the spirit into perfect submission to the will of God, and delivers from everything like a rebellious heart or a critical spirit. Prayer sanctifies trouble to our highest good.

Prayer so prepares the heart that it softens under the disciplining hand of God.

Prayer allows God to freely work with us and in us in the day of trouble. Prayer lifts our burdens and brings to us the sweetest, the highest and greatest good.

Prayer permits God's servant – trouble – to accomplish its mission in us, with us, and for us.

Dear Father, help me to see that my prayers allow You to work freely with me and in me in the day of trouble. Amen.

A Positive Spirit

"Because he loves Me," says the LORD, "I will rescue him;
I will protect him, for he acknowledges My name.
He will call upon Me, and I will answer him; I will be
with him in trouble, I will deliver him and honor him."
Psalm 91:14-15

The end of trouble is always good in the mind of God. If trouble fails in its mission, it is either because of a lack of prayer or unbelief, or both. The good or evil of trouble is always determined by the spirit in which it is received.

Trouble proves a blessing or a curse, depending on how it is received and treated by us. It either softens or hardens us. It either draws us to prayer and to God or drives us away.

The sun can either soften the wax or harden the clay. The sun can either melt the ice or dry out moisture from the earth.

Dear God, please grant me a positive spirit so that I will see the end of trouble as good. I want my troubles to be a blessing and not a curse. In Jesus' name I pray. Amen.

May 23

God's Promises

"Test Me in this" says the Lord Almighty.
Malachi 3:10

God's great promises find their fulfillment along the lines of prayer.

In this connection, let it be noted that God's promises are always personal and specific. They deal with people. Each believer can claim the promise as his own. God deals with each one personally, so that every person can put the promises to the test.

The praying saint has the right to put his hand upon God's promises and claim them as his own, made especially for him and intended to embrace all his needs, both present and future.

God Almighty, I claim Your promises in Your Word as my own today. Thank You that You always keep Your promises. Amen.

The Promised Messiah

"Your prayer has been heard."
Luke 1:13

God had promised through His prophets that the coming Messiah would have a forerunner. How many homes and wombs in Israel had longed for this great honor?

Perhaps Zechariah and Elizabeth were the only ones who realized this great dignity and blessing by praying for it.

It was then that the Word of the Lord, as spoken by the prophets, and the prayers of Zechariah and his wife brought John the Baptist into the withered womb and into the childless home of Zechariah and Elizabeth.

Thank You, dear Father, for always keeping Your promises. Amen.

Make the Promise Real!

*I urge you, brothers, by our Lord Jesus Christ
and by the love of the Spirit, to join me
in my struggle by praying to God for me.*
Romans 15:30

How did Paul make this promise efficient? How did
he make the promise real? Here is the answer. Paul
asked his brothers in Christ to pray for him.

Their prayers, united with his prayer, were to
secure his deliverance and secure his safety, and
were also to make the apostolic promise vital and
cause it to be fully realized.

All is to be sanctified and realized by the Word
of God and prayer. God's deep and wide river of
promise will be life-giving waters to our hearts.

*Father, You want us to unite with other believers
to make Your promises real and efficient. Guide me in
requesting my fellow believers to pray for me. Amen.*

God Gives Nothing by Halves

"In that day you will no longer ask Me anything.
I tell you the truth, My Father will give
you whatever you ask in My name. Ask and you
will receive, and your joy will be complete."
John 16:23-24

God has committed Himself to us by His Word through our prayers. The Word of God is the basis, the inspiration, and the heart of prayer.

Jesus Christ stands as the illustration of God's Word and its unlimited goodness in promise as well as in realization. God takes nothing by halves. He gives nothing by halves. We can have the whole of Him when He has the whole of us.

These often-heard promises seem to daze us, and instead of allowing them to move us to asking and receiving, we turn away full of wonder, but empty-handed and with empty hearts.

Dear God, You commit the whole of Yourself to us. You give nothing by halves. I want to give my all to You. Amen.

May 27

Specific Answers to Prayers

"Call to Me and I will answer you."
Jeremiah 33:3

God the Father and Jesus Christ, His Son, are both strongly committed by the truth of the Word and by the integrity of their character to answer prayer.

Not only does this and all the promises pledge God to answer prayer, but they assure us that the answer will be specific.

Our Lord's invariable teaching was that we will receive whatever we ask for in prayer. If we ask for bread, He will give us bread. If we ask for an egg, He will give us an egg. Evil will not be given to us in answer to prayer, rather God's goodness.

Almighty God, thank You for answering our prayers specifically like we request. Amen.

A Compassionate Savior

We have one who has been tempted in
every way, just as we are – yet was without sin.
Hebrews 4:15

Jesus Christ was altogether man. He was the divine Son of God, yet at the same time He was the human Son of God.

This allowed our Lord to be a compassionate Savior. It is no sin to feel the pain and realize the darkness on the path into which God leads us. It is only human to cry out against the pain and desolation of the hour.

How strong it makes us to have one True North to guide us to the glory of God!

Lord God, thank You that because You have been tempted in every way while on earth, You understand our struggles perfectly. I look to You as my guiding light. Amen.

May 29

Our Heavenly Father

"If you, then, though you are evil, know how to give good gifts to your children, how much more will your Father in heaven give good gifts to those who ask Him!"
Matthew 7:11

Earthly parents give when asked and respond to the crying of their children. The encouragement to pray is transferred from our earthly father to our heavenly Father – from the weak to the omnipotent. Our heavenly Father is the highest conception of fatherhood.

He will supply all our needs, more than our earthly fathers can, and He will enable us to meet every difficult duty and fulfill every law. Though it may be hard for our flesh and blood to do, it is made easy under the full supply of our Father's divine and everlasting help.

Dear Father God, You are the perfect and divine example of fatherhood. I thank You for supplying all my needs. Amen.

May 30

God Cannot Lie

A faith and knowledge resting on the hope
of eternal life, which God, who does not lie,
promised before the beginning of time.
Titus 1:2

God explicitly says: There are no limitations, no hedges, no hindrances in the way of Me fulfilling My promises. Man is to look for the answer, be inspired by the expectation of the answer, and demand the answer with humble boldness.

God, who cannot lie, is bound to answer. The people of God in biblical times were unshaken in their faith in the absolute certainty that God would fulfill His promises to them. They rested in security on the Word of God.

Thus, their history is marked by repeated asking and receiving at the hands of God.

Sovereign God, I know that there are no hindrances, limitations or hedges in You fulfilling Your promises. You are Truth. I praise Your name. Amen.

May 31

June

Hold on, Press on and Wait

*Jesus told His disciples a parable to show them
that they should always pray and not give up.*
Luke 18:1

The parable that comes after the words above was taught with the intention of saving people from faintheartedness in prayer. Our Lord wanted to teach us to guard against negligence, and encourage us to show persistence.

Persistent prayer is a mighty move of the soul toward God. It is the ability to hold on, press on, and wait. Restless desire, restful patience, and strength to hold on are all embraced in it.

It is not merely a routine, but a passion of soul. It is not something half-needed, but a sheer necessity.

Dear Father, save me from faint-heartedness when I pray. Teach me persistence and the ability to hold on, press on and wait. Amen.

June 1

Wrestling in Prayer

The prayer of a righteous man is powerful and effective.
James 5:16

Wrestling in persistent prayer does not mean physical violence or fleshly energy. It is an inward force or ability planted and inspired by the Holy Spirit. In effect, it is the intercession of the Spirit of God in us.

The divine Spirit supplies us with the energy of His own determination. This is the essence of the persistence that urges our praying to continue until the blessings descend.

This wrestling in prayer is not loud, but firm and urgent. When there are no visible outlets for its mighty forces, it may be silent.

Dear God, thank You for Your Holy Spirit who intercedes for us when we wrestle in prayer. Amen.

Tribulation, Suffering and Affliction

"In this world you will have trouble.
But take heart! I have overcome the world!"
John 16:33

In the New Testament there are three words used that mean trouble. They are tribulation, suffering and affliction. These words differ somewhat, and yet, each of them means trouble of some kind.

Our Lord told His disciples to expect tribulation in this life, teaching them that tribulation belongs to this world; that they could not hope to escape it, and that they would not be carried through this life on flowery beds of comfort.

This is a hard lesson to learn. We can, however, take heart, because God has overcome the world. Through Him, we are victors.

Lord, I rejoice in Your name. Although we will face troubles of many kinds, we can be sure that You will carry us through them because You have already overcome this world. Amen.

June 3

Continual Prayer

Be joyful always; pray continually;
give thanks in all circumstances,
for this is God's will for you in Christ Jesus.
1 Thessalonians 5:16-18.

Nothing distinguishes the children of God so clearly and strongly as prayer. It is the one infallible mark and test of being a Christian. But even the Christian has to cultivate *continual* prayer. It must be habitual, but it must be much more than just a habit.

It is a duty, one that rises far above the ordinary implications of the term. It is the expression of a relationship with God, a yearning for divine communion.

It is the flow of the soul toward its original fountain. It is a statement of the soul's origin, a claiming of sonship that links man to the eternal.

Almighty God, I want to be distinguished as Your child through my prayers to You. My soul yearns to come into Your presence every day. Amen.

June 4

The Horizon of Hope

"These in white robes – who are they, and where did they come from?" And he said, "These are they who have come out of the great tribulation; they have washed their robes and made them white in the blood of the Lamb. And God will wipe away every tear from their eyes."
Revelation 7:13-14, 17

Trouble makes the earth undesirable and creates a desire for heaven within us. There where trouble never comes. It is the path of tribulation that leads to that world.

Hear John as he talked about it and those who will be there. Children of God, you who have suffered, who have been greatly tried, whose sad experiences have often produced broken spirits and bleeding hearts, cheer up!

God is in all your troubles, you just have to be patient, submissive and consistent in prayer.

Father God, in this world I've experienced suffering. Please help me to be patient, submissive and prayerful, for You are in all my troubles. Thank You, Lord. Amen.

June 5

Persistence

*You know that the testing
of your faith develops perseverance.*
James 1:3

Persistence is the pressing of our desires on God with urgency and perseverance. It is praying with courage until our cries are heard.

The man who has an intimate relationship with God appreciates his privilege of approaching God in prayer.

Prayer that influences God is said to be the out-pouring of the fervent, effectual righteous man. It is prayer on fire.

It does not have a feeble, flickering flame or a momentary spark, but shines with a vigorous, steady glow.

Dear God, I want my prayers to be effectual. Ignite my spirit with the vigorous, steady glow of Your presence so that my prayers may bring You glory. Amen.

June 6

Moses, Elijah and Jesus

*Then Jesus told His disciples a parable to show them
that they should always pray and not give up.*
Luke 18:1

Moses prayed for forty days and forty nights to stop
the wrath of God. His example is an encouragement
to present-day faith in its darkest hour.

Elijah repeated his prayer seven times before the
rain clouds appeared on the horizon.

During His earthly life, the blessed Savior spent
many nights in prayer. In Gethsemane He present-
ed the same petition three times with unshaken, yet
submissive persistence. This called on every part
of His soul and brought about tears and bloody
sweat.

Jesus' life victories were all won in hours of persistent prayer. He taught, by example, the importance of consistent prayer.

*Dear Father, thank You for Jesus' example of pray-
ing day and night and not giving up. Amen.*

God Rewards Abundantly

And the Lord said, "Listen to what the unjust judge says. And will not God bring about justice for His chosen ones, who cry out to Him day and night? I tell you, He will see that they get justice, and quickly. However, when the Son of Man comes, will He find faith on the earth?"
Luke 18:6-8

He who does not push his plea does not pray at all. Prayers with no heart have no claim on heaven and no hearing in the courts above. God waits patiently as His people cry to Him day and night. He is moved by their requests a thousand times more than this unjust judge was.

Waiting for answers to prayer is limited by persistent praying, and the answer is richly given. God sees His praying child's faith. He honors this faith that stays and cries by persisting in prayer, so that it is strengthened and enriched. Then He rewards it abundantly.

Thank You, Lord, for richly rewarding persistent praying. Thank You for seeing my faith when I pray. Amen.

June 8

Successful Persistence

"Lord, help me!"
Matthew 15:25

The Canaanite woman, who came to Jesus on behalf of her daughter, is a notable instance of successful persistence. It is one that is highly encouraging to all who pray successfully. Her heart was in her prayer.

At first, Jesus appears to pay no attention to her agony and ignores her cry for relief. She came closer, cutting her prayer in half, and fell at His feet. Worshiping Him, she made her daughter's case known.

This last cry won her case. Her daughter was healed that same hour.

Hopeful, urgent, and unwearied, she stayed near the Master, insisting and praying until the answer was given. What an example of persistence!

Almighty God, I want to pray persistently, like the Canaanite woman. In worship I make my case known to You. Amen.

Clinging Faith

"Woman, you have great faith!
Your request is granted."
Matthew 15:28

The Canaanite woman gives a glimpse of her cling-ing faith, and her spiritual insight. The Master went to the Sidonian country so that this truth could be shown for all time: There is no cry as effective as persistent prayer, and there is no prayer to which God surrenders Himself so fully and so freely.

The persistence of this distressed mother brought about her request. Instead of being an offense to the Savior, it drew from Him a word of wonder and glad surprise.

Dear Lord God, please increase my faith and help me to pray persistently. Amen.

Sufferings

I consider that our present sufferings are not worth comparing with the glory that will be revealed in us.
Romans 8:18

Paul used the word *sufferings* to describe the troubles of life in the comforting passage where he contrasted life's troubles to the final glory of heaven, which shall be the reward of all who patiently endure until the end.

Further, he spoke of the afflictions that come to the people of God in this world, and he regarded them as nearly weightless when compared to the weight of glory awaiting all who are submissive, patient and faithful in all their troubles.

God, make me a patient and faithful servant so that Your glory may be revealed in me. Amen.

Afflictions

For our light and momentary troubles are achieving
for us an eternal glory that far outweighs them all.
2 Corinthians 4:17

Afflictions can work for us only if we co-operate with God in prayer. God can accomplish His highest ends for us through prayer. His providence works best when His people pray. They know that trouble serves a purpose. They know that God can use trouble to strengthen their relationship with Him.

The greatest value in trouble comes to those who turn to God in prayer. In fact, the only way to endure trouble patiently, is to pray consistently.

The school of prayer is where patience is learned and practiced.

Almighty God, I want to learn from my troubles. I bow before You in prayer. Amen.

A Chain of Graces

*We rejoice in our sufferings, because we know that
suffering produces perseverance; perseverance, character;
and character, hope. And hope does not disappoint us,
because God has poured out His love into our
hearts by the Holy Spirit, whom He has given us.*
Romans 5:3-5

Prayer brings us into that state of grace where suffering cannot only be endured, but where there is a spirit of rejoicing over it. What a chain of graces that could flow from tribulation.

It is in the furnace that faith is tested, patience is tried, and where all those rich virtues are developed that make up Christian character.

It is while they are passing through deep waters that God shows how close He can come to His praying, believing saints.

Father, thank You for drawing close to us when we need You most. When we go through deep waters, Your presence comes very close to us. Amen.

Molding the Soul

*Therefore we do not lose heart. Though
outwardly we are wasting away, yet inwardly
we are being renewed day by day.*
2 Corinthians 4:16

Prayer has everything to do with molding the soul into the image of God. It has everything to do with enriching, broadening, and maturing the soul's experience of God.

A man who does not pray cannot possibly be called a Christian.

Prayer is the only way the soul can enter into fellowship and communion with the Source of all Christlike spirit and energy. Therefore, if he does not pray, he is not of the household of faith.

Dear God, I thank You that I can enter into fellowship and communion with You through my prayers. Amen.

An All-wise Designer

Be joyful in hope, patient in affliction, faithful in prayer.
Romans 12:12

God's highest aim in dealing with His people is to develop a Christian character in them. He is seeking to make us like Himself. God wants to create in us a spirit of patience, meekness, and submission to His will. He wants us to carry everything to Him in prayer.

And trouble in any form tends to do this very thing, for this is the end and aim of trouble. This is its work.

It is not a chance incident in life, but has a design in view, just as it has an all-wise Designer. God uses trouble to draw us closer to Him.

O Lord, I know that You shape my character through suffering. Please help me to be joyful always, and patient in affliction. Amen.

Trouble Attracts Attention

*"When he came to his senses, he said,
'How many of my father's hired men have food
to spare, and here I am starving to death!'"*
Luke 15:17

Just as prayer is wide in its range, so trouble is infinitely varied in its uses. Trouble is sometimes used to attract attention and to stop people in the busy rush of life.

The prodigal son was independent and self-sufficient when it went well with him. But, when money and friends departed, he decided to return to his father's house.

Through trouble many a man who has forgotten God has been stopped, caused to consider his ways, and brought to remember God and pray. Blessed is trouble when it accomplishes this in people's lives!

Dear God, use my troubles to let me consider my ways, bring me back to praying and fix my eyes on You. Amen.

The Possibilities of Prayer

Open wide your mouth and I will fill it.
Psalm 81:10

How vast are the possibilities of prayer! It lays its hand on God Almighty and moves Him to do what He would not otherwise do if prayer were not offered.

Prayer is a wonderful power placed by God in the hands of His people, which may be used to accomplish great purposes and to achieve unusual results.

Prayer reaches to everything, taking in all things great and small that are promised by God to His children.

O Father, I thank You for the wonderful power of prayer that You placed in our hands. Amen.

Prayer Proves Itself

"If any one chooses to do God's will, he will find out whether My teaching comes from God."
John 7:17

The records of the achievements of prayer are encouraging to faith.

Prayer is no untried theory. Prayer is a divine arrangement from God; designed for the benefit of mankind, intended as a means for furthering the interests of His cause on earth, and carrying out His gracious purposes in redemption and providence. Prayer proves itself. It is capable of proving its virtue through those who pray. Prayer needs no proof other than its accomplishments.

If any man wants to know the virtue of prayer, if he wants to know what it can achieve, let him pray. Let him put prayer to the test.

Dear Lord God, thank You that prayer is no untried theory. It is a divine arrangement from You for our benefit, and for carrying out Your plans on earth for Your glory. Amen.

A Soul Set Alight for God

Pray for us, too, that God
may open a door for our message.
Colossians 4:3

How vast are the possibilities of prayer! What great things are accomplished by this divinely appointed means of grace! It is the breathing of a soul inflamed for God and inflamed for man.

Prayer opens possibilities for the spread of the gospel. Prayer moves God to do His work in new and enlarged ways. Prayer not only gives great power, it also helps you to spread the gospel.

Prayer makes the gospel move with glorious speed. It moves with God's power and with saintly swiftness.

God, I know that through prayer I can open doors for the mighty work of Your Spirit to spread the Good News. Please help me to never grow weary in prayer. Amen.

Go Gospel Go!

Brothers, pray for us that the message of
the Lord may spread rapidly and be honored.
2 Thessalonians 3:1

The gospel moves altogether too slowly, often timidly, and with feeble steps. What will make this gospel move rapidly, like an athlete in a race? The answer is at hand.

Prayer, more prayer and better prayer will do the deed. This means of grace will give swiftness, splendor, and divinity to the gospel. The possibilities of prayer reach to all things.

Whatever concerns man's welfare and whatever has to do with God's plans and purposes concerning people on earth can be a subject for prayer.

Dear Father God, I want to help move Your message faster to all people. Guide me through Your Spirit to pray always and about all things. Amen.

Whatever

*"I will do whatever you ask in My name, so that
the Son may bring glory to the Father. You may ask
Me for anything in My name, and I will do it."*
John 14:13-14

"Whatever you ask" embraces all that concerns
God's praying people. And whatever is left out
of "whatever" is left out of prayer. Where will we
draw the lines that will leave out or limit the word
"whatever"?

Define it, and search out and publish the things
that the word does not include. If "whatever" does
not include all things, then substitute the word with
"anything".

The possibilities of prayer are unspeakable, but
who has learned the lesson of prayer; who realizes
and measures up to these possibilities?

*Dear God, thank You that we can pray to You about
anything. Amen.*

Increased Praying

*"I tell you the truth, My Father will
give you whatever you ask in My name."*
John 16:23

Here is a very definite catchphrase from our Lord
to increase our praying. We are definitely urged by
Him to ask for large things, and the dignity and so-
lemnity of this announcement is indicated by the
phrase, "I tell you the truth."

Why are these words recorded in this last and vital conversation of our Lord with His disciples? The
answer is that our Lord wanted to prepare them for
the new dispensation in which prayer was to have
marvelous results and be the chief agency to con-
serve and make His gospel flourish.

*Father God, I want my prayers to You to make the
gospel flourish. Please guide me when I pray so that
Your name may be glorified. Amen.*

The Fruit of Prayer

"You did not choose Me, but I chose you and appointed you to go and bear fruit – fruit that will last. Then the Father will give you whatever you ask in My name."
John 15:16

In our Lord's generous statement to His disciples about choosing them so that they would bear fruit, He clearly teaches that this matter of praying and fruit bearing is not a petty business of our choice.

He specifically had our praying in mind; He has chosen us of His own divine selection; and He expects us to do this one thing of praying, and to do it well.

The main objective of choosing us as His disciples and of sharing friendship with Him was that we might be better fitted to bear the fruit of prayer.

O God, You have chosen me of Your own divine selection. I want to do what You require from us – to pray, and to do it well. Amen.

God Answers Prayer

"Everything is possible for him who believes."
Mark 9:23

We affirm with absolute certainty that God answers prayer. He hears and answers every prayer where the true conditions of praying are met. This is either true or not. If not, then there is nothing in prayer. Then prayer becomes but the recitation of words.

But if what the Scripture verse says is true, then there are vast possibilities in prayer. Then it is far-reaching in its scope and wide in its range.

Then it is true that prayer can lay its hand upon God Almighty and move Him to do great and wonderful things.

Almighty Father, I believe that everything is possible for those who believe in You. Thank You that our prayers can move You to do great things. Amen.

June 24

Prayer Can Move the World

"In everything ... present your requests to God."
Philippians 4:6

Prayer is a direct address to God. Prayer secures blessings and betters people because it reaches the ear of God.

Prayer affects people by affecting God. Prayer moves people because it moves God to move them. Prayer moves the hand that moves the world.

The utmost possibilities of prayer have rarely been realized. The promises of God are so great to those who truly pray, that when He puts Himself fully into the hands of the praying ones, it almost staggers our faith and leaves us amazed.

Dear Lord God, thank You that our prayers secure blessings and make people better because they reach Your ears. Amen.

God Means What He Says

*The hope of eternal life, which God, who does not
lie, promised before the beginning of time.*
Titus 1:2

Let us always keep in mind and never for one moment allow ourselves to doubt the statement that God means what He says in all His promises. God's promises are His own Word.

Unfortunately we have failed to express ourselves fully in prayer. The ability to pray can be secured by the grace and power of the Holy Spirit, but it demands such a strenuous and noble character that it is a rare thing for a man or woman to be on praying ground and on pleading terms with God.

Dear God, through the grace, mercy and power of Your Holy Spirit our ability to pray can be secured. I thank You, Lord. Amen.

The Twins: Prayer and Faith

"For He who promised is faithful."
Hebrews 10:23

The possibilities of prayer are the possibilities of faith. Prayer and faith are Siamese twins. One heart brings them both to life. Faith is always praying; prayer is always believing. Faith must have a tongue by which it can speak; prayer is the tongue of faith. Faith must receive; prayer is the hand of faith stretched out to receive.

Prayer must rise and soar; faith must give prayer the wings to fly and ascend. Prayer must have an audience with God; faith opens the door and an audience is given. Prayer asks; faith lays its hand on the thing asked for.

Father God, through my faith in You I am moved to pray, and through my prayers I believe that You can do immeasurably more than we can ask or imagine. Amen.

The Sum of Religion

"Nothing will be impossible for you."
Matthew 17:20

Prayer is not an indifferent, small thing. It is not a sweet little privilege. It is a great prerogative, far-reaching in its effects. Failure to pray entails great loss. Prayer is not just an episode of the Christian life.

Life is a preparation for and the result of prayer. In its condition, prayer is the sum of religion.

Prayer is not only the language of spiritual life, but prayer also makes its very essence and forms its innermost, real character.

God, thank You for granting us the great privilege of prayer that has far-reaching effects. Amen.

The Gift of Anointment

For it is by grace you have been saved, through faith –
and this not from yourselves, it is the gift of God.
Ephesians 2:8

It is an anointed preacher who stirs many congregations.

It belongs to the experience of the man as well as to his preaching. It is that which transforms him into the image of his divine Master, as well as that by which he declares the truths of Christ with power.

This anointing is not a fixed gift. It is a conditional gift. This anointing comes directly from God in answer to prayer. Prayer, much prayer, is the price of anointment.

Without perseverance in prayer, the anointing, like over-kept manna, breeds worms.

Dear Father, I want to receive Your gift of anointing. I know that this anointing comes directly from You in answer to prayer. Please help me persevere in prayer. Amen.

The Divine Comforter

*The Spirit intercedes for the saints
in accordance with God's will.*
Romans 8:27

The Comforter plants Himself not in the mountain, but in the middle of the human heart, to rouse it to the struggle and to teach it the need of prayer.

The Divine Comforter puts the burden of earth's need into human hearts and makes human lips give voice to their unutterable groaning!

What a mighty Christ of prayer is the Holy Spirit! How He quenches every flame in the heart but the flame of heavenly desire! How He quiets, like a weaned child, all the self-will, until we pray only as He prays.

Father, I thank You that Your Spirit intercedes for us in accordance to Your will. What a mighty God we serve. Amen.

July

Prayer That Motivates God

*Then He said to them, "Suppose one of you has a friend,
and he goes to him at midnight and says, 'Friend, lend me
three loaves of bread, because a friend of mine on a journey
has come to me, and I have nothing to set before him.'"*
Luke 11:5-6

The purpose of Christ's teachings is to declare that
His followers are to pray earnestly.

All these qualities of the soul are brought out in
the parable of the man who went to his friend for
bread at midnight. This man did his task with confidence. He could not go back empty-handed. The
flat refusal shamed and surprised him. Here even
friendship failed! But there was still something to
be tried – stern resolution and fixed determination.

He would stay and pursue his demand until the
door was opened. He proceeded to do this and, by
persistence, secured what ordinary requesting had
failed to obtain.

*Dear Father, thank You for teaching us through Your
Word that persistence in prayer yields results. Amen.*

July 1

An Act of Holiness

Make every effort to live in peace with all men and to be holy; without holiness no one will see the Lord.
Hebrews 12:14

Unfortunately, we have substituted the external for the internal. Even in the church, we are much further advanced in material matters than in spiritual matters.

It is largely due to the decline of prayer. With the decline of the work of holiness has come the decline of the business of praying. We may excuse it, yet it is all too clear that the emphasis in the work of the present-day church is not on prayer.

The church is not producing praying men and women, because the church is not intently engaged in this one great work of holiness.

Dear God, I pray that our church will engage again in the act of holiness. I pray that our church will produce praying men and women for Your glory. Amen.

Forceless Prayers

Those who know Your name will trust in You,
for You, LORD, have never forsaken those who seek You.
Psalm 9:10

Persistent prayer is the earnest, inward movement of the heart toward God. Isaiah lamented that no one stirred himself to take hold of God. There was much praying done in Isaiah's time, but it was indifferent and self-righteous.

There were no mighty moves of souls toward God. There was no array of sanctified energies bent on reaching God. There was no energy to draw the treasures of His grace from Him.

Forceless prayers have no power to overcome difficulties, get results, or gain complete victories. We must win God before we can win our plea.

Dear Lord God, I want my prayers to be forceful. I want my prayers to be an inward movement of my heart toward You so that You will be glorified by them. Amen.

Persistent Prayer is Powerful

In the last days the mountain of the LORD's temple will be established as chief among the mountains; it will be raised above the hills, and all nations will stream to it.
Isaiah 2:2

Isaiah looked with hopeful eyes to the day when faith would flourish and there would be times of real praying. Times in which our prayers would keep all spiritual interests busy and make increasing demands on God's exhaustless treasures.

Persistent prayer never hesitates or grows weary. It is never discouraged. It never yields to cowardice, but is lifted up and sustained by a hope that knows no despair and a faith that will not let go.

Persistent prayer has patience to wait and strength to continue. It never prepares itself to quit praying, and it refuses to get up from its knees until an answer is received.

Keep me on my knees, Almighty God, until my prayers are answered. Thank You, Lord. Amen.

Ask, Seek and Knock

"Ask and it will be given to you; seek and you will find; knock and the door will be opened to you."
Matthew 7:7

These are the ringing challenges of our Lord regarding prayer. These challenges are His explanation that true praying must wait and advance in effort and urgency until the prayer is answered.

In the three words *ask, seek* and *knock,* Jesus, by the order in which He places them, urges the necessity of persistence in prayer. Asking, seeking, and knocking are ascending rungs in the ladder of successful prayer.

No principle is more definitely enforced by Christ than that successful prayer must contain the qualities of waiting and persevering.

Father God, I want the qualities that waits and perseveres to be in my prayers. Please guide me as I ask, seek and knock when I pray. Amen.

Keep on Praying

As Jesus went on from there, two blind men followed Him, calling out, "Have mercy on us, Son of David!"
Matthew 9:27

The most important qualities in Christ's estimate of the highest form of praying are unbeatable courage and stability of purpose.

Even if God does not answer our prayers right away, we must keep on praying. In Matthew we have the first record of the miracle of healing the blind. We have an illustration of how our Lord did not seem to hear immediately those who sought Him. But the two blind men continued with their petitions. He did not answer them and went into the house.

The needy ones followed Him and, finally, gained their eyesight and their plea.

Almighty God, I pray for courage and stability of purpose to persevere until my prayers are answered. Amen.

The Case of the Blind Bartimaeus

When he heard that it was Jesus of Nazareth, he began to shout, "Jesus, Son of David, have mercy on me!"
Mark 10:47

The case of the blind Bartimaeus is noteworthy in many ways.

At first, Jesus seemed not to hear. The crowd rebuked the noisy babbling of Bartimaeus. Despite the apparent unconcern of our Lord and the rebuke of an impatient crowd, the blind beggar still cried out. He increased the loudness of his cry until Jesus was moved.

Finally, the crowd, as well as Jesus, listened and spoke in favor of his cause. He won his case. His persistence won where half-hearted indifference would surely have failed.

Dear Lord, have mercy on me, a sinner. I ask this in Jesus' name. Amen.

July 7

The Necessity of Persistence

On reaching the place, He said to them, "Pray that you will not fall into temptation."
Luke 22:40

Faith functions in connection with prayer and persistence. Persistence cultivates the believe that prayer will be answered. A person with a persistent spirit will be blessed.

The absolute necessity of persistent prayer is plainly stated in the Word of God and needs to be restated today. Love of ease, spiritual laziness, and religious indifference all operate against this type of petitioning.

Our praying, however, needs to be coaxed with an energy that never tires. It needs to have a persistency that will not be denied and a courage that never fails.

Dear Lord God, inspire my praying with an energy that never tires so that I can come to the place where my faith takes hold of Your blessings. Amen.

A Season of Persistent Prayer

*Moses sought the favor of the LORD his God.
"O LORD," he said, "why should Your anger burn
against Your people, whom You brought out of
Egypt with great power and a mighty hand?"*
Exodus 32:11

Moses furnished us with an excellent example of persistence in prayer. Instead of allowing his intimacy with God to release him from the necessity for persistence, he regarded it as an important aspect of prayer.

When Israel set up the golden calf, the wrath of God increased fiercely against them. Jehovah, bent on executing justice, told Moses what He intended to do. But Moses would not accept the verdict. He threw himself down before the Lord in an agony of intercession on behalf of the sinning Israelites.

For forty days and forty nights he fasted and prayed. What a season of persistent prayer that was!

Dear Father, thank You for Moses' example of what it means to pray persistently. Amen.

Delays and Denials

*We, who with unveiled faces all reflect the Lord's glory,
are being transformed into His likeness with ever-increasing
glory, which comes from the Lord, who is the Spirit.*
2 Corinthians 3:18

We need to give thought to the mysterious fact of prayer – the certainty that there will be delays and denials. We must prepare for and permit these delays and denials.

The praying Christian is like a brave soldier who, as the conflict grows more severe, exhibits more courage. When delay and denial come, he increases his earnest asking and does not stop until prayer prevails.

There can be no question about persistent prayer moving God and improving human character. If we were more in agreement with God in the command of intercession, our faces would shine more brightly.

God, help me to wait patiently for Your answers to my prayers. I know that through making me wait You strengthen my character. Amen.

July 10

What Is God's Work in This World?

The reason the Son of God appeared
was to destroy the devil's work.
1 John 3:8

God has a great task on hand in this world. This task is involved in the plan of salvation. It embraces redemption and providence.

What, then, is God's work in this world? God's work is to make the hearts and lives of His children holy. Man is a fallen creature, born with an evil nature. God's entire plan is to take hold of fallen man and to seek to change him and make him holy.

God's work is to make holy soldiers out of unholy people. This is the very reason Christ came into the world.

Dear Father, take hold of me, a fallen person. Change me, and make me holy. Amen.

The Aim of All Christian Effort

Just as He who called you is holy, so be holy in all you do; for it is written: "Be holy, because I am holy."
1 Peter 1:15-16

God is holy in nature and in all His ways, and He wants to make man like Himself. He wants man to be Christlike. This is the aim of all Christian effort. We must therefore constantly and earnestly pray to be made holy.

Not that we are to *do* holy, but rather to *be* holy. Being must precede doing. First be, then do. First obtain a holy heart, then live a holy life. And for this high and gracious end, God has made the most ample provisions in the atoning work of our Lord and through the agency of the Holy Spirit.

Dear God, I want to be more like You every day. I want to be holy like You are holy. Make my heart holy so that I can live a life pleasing to You. Amen.

Preaching by Example

Like newborn babies, crave pure spiritual milk,
so that by it you may grow up in your salvation.
1 Peter 2:2

The work of God in the world is the perfection of holiness in His people. Keep this in mind. But we might ask: Is this work advancing in the church?

The present-day church owns the latest technological equipment. The church must, however, not lose sight of its most important purpose, namely to lead people to live holy lives through prayer. Ministers, like laymen, must be holy in life, in conversation and in temper.

They must be examples to the flock of God in all things. By their lives they are to preach as well as reflect the image of our Lord.

Father, I want to reflect Your image to the world.
Please guide me through the help of Your precious Holy
Spirit. Amen.

July 13

Business Integrity

The Lord detests men of perverse heart but He delights in those whose ways are blameless.
Proverbs 11:20

Again let us ask: Are our leading laymen examples of holiness? Does business integrity and honesty run parallel with religious activity and Christian observance?

If God's work is to make men and women holy – and He has made ample provisions in the law of doing this very thing – why should it be thought impertinent and useless to express such personal and pointed questions such as these?

They deal directly with the work of God and with its progress and its perfection. These questions go to the very center of the disease. They hit the spot.

Dear God, You chose me to be holy and blameless in Your sight, even before Creation. Please help me, Lord, to live a life pleasing to You. Amen.

Material vs. Spiritual Prosperity

"For where your treasure is,
there your heart will be also."
Matthew 6:21

Material prosperity is not a sign of spiritual prosperity. It may easily blind the eyes of church leaders, so much so that they will make it a substitute for spiritual prosperity. We must be careful not to do this.

Financial prosperity does not signify growth in holiness. The seasons of material prosperity are rarely seasons of spiritual advance, either to the individual or to the church. It is so easy to lose sight of God when wealth increases. It is so easy to lean on human agencies and cease praying and relying upon God when material prosperity comes to the church.

Focus your eyes on God to ensure that your spirit will grow in holiness.

O God, I know that I sometimes lose sight of You when things go well with me. I pray that my spirit will grow and prosper in holiness. Amen.

July 15

Outpouring of the Holy Spirit

Surely the arm of the LORD is not too
short to save, nor His ear too dull to hear.
Isaiah 59:1

If the work of God is progressing and we are growing in holiness, then some perplexing questions arise. If the church is making advances on the lines of deep spirituality – if we are praying people, and if our people are hungering after holiness, why do we have so few mighty outpourings of the Holy Spirit?

There is only one answer for this state of things. We have cultivated other things, to the neglect of the work of holiness. We have permitted our minds to be preoccupied with material things in the church. We need to focus our eyes on the Lord so that He can pour His Spirit out on us.

Almighty God, I sometimes keep myself occupied with unimportant matters instead of focusing my thoughts and actions on You. Guide me in Your truth today. Amen.

The Work of God

*He will be an instrument for noble purposes, made holy,
useful to the Master and prepared to do any good work.*
2 Timothy 2:21

People who dedicate themselves to the work of God
must focus on the giving and receiving of grace and
not on the receiving of gifts. A full supply of grace
brings an increase of gifts.

It may be stressed that no results, a low experience, and pointless, powerless preaching always
flow from a lack of grace. And a lack of grace flows
from a lack of praying.

Great grace comes from great praying. In carrying out His great work in the world, God works
through human agents. He works through His
church collectively and through His people individually.

*Dear God, make me a holy instrument for Your
noble purposes. Make me useful and prepare me to do
any good work for Your glory. Amen.*

July 17

Recognized by our Fruit

"Thus, by their fruit you will recognize them."
Matthew 7:20

The world judges religion not by what the Bible says, but by how Christians live. Christians are the Bible that sinners read. The emphasis, then, is placed on holiness of life. In selecting church workers, the quality of holiness is not considered.

Prayer may seem insignificant in the eyes of the world, but it is important in all of God's movements and in all of His plans. He looks for holy people, those noted for their praying habits. As a child of God, bear fruit in such a way that the world may see to whom you belong.

Ask the Spirit of God to guide you to a more holy life.

Father God, I want to bear good fruit so that the world can see to whom I belong. Guide me to a more holy life. In Jesus' name. Amen.

Spiritual Quality

Do not be deceived: God cannot be mocked.
A man reaps what he sows.
Galatians 6:7

We might wonder why so little is accomplished in the world for the great work that God has in hand. The fact is that it is surprising that so much has been done through people with such weak faith.

Let it be said again and again that holiness of life is the divine standard of religion. Nothing short of this will satisfy the divine requirement. People can do many good things and yet not be holy in heart and righteous in conduct. They can do many good things and yet lack that spiritual quality of the heart called holiness.

Strive towards higher spiritual quality and holiness through Christ Jesus, so that He can use you to do His great work on earth.

O Lord, I want You to use me to do great things for You. I want my actions and my heart to speak of righteousness before You. Please guide me. Amen.

Pray Until the Answer Comes

"So I say to you: Ask and it will be given to you; seek and you will find; knock and the door will be opened to you. For everyone who asks receives; he who seeks finds; and to him who knocks, the door will be opened."
Luke 11:9-10

The success of the persistent man in the face of a flat denial (Luke 11:5-8), was used by the Savior to illustrate the need for perseverance in humble prayer before the throne of heavenly grace.

When the answer is not immediately given, the praying Christian must gather courage at each delay. He must urgently go forward until the answer comes. The answer is assured, if he has the faith to press his petition with vigorous faith.

Negligence, impatience, and fear will be fatal to our prayers. The Father's heart, hand and infinite willingness to hear and give to His children is waiting for the start of our perseverance.

Strengthen my faith, Lord God, so that I will gather courage to press on toward a more holy life. Amen.

Pray and Be Prayed For

*I urge you, brothers, by our Lord Jesus Christ
and by the love of the Spirit, to join me
in my struggle by praying to God for me.*
Romans 15:30

For the preacher, prayer is not simply the duty of his profession, but a privilege. It is a necessity. Air is not more necessary to the lungs than prayer is to the preacher. The preacher must pray; the preacher must be prayed for. These two propositions are wedded into a union that should never be separated.

It will take all the praying he can do, to meet the fearful responsibilities and success in his great work. The true preacher realizes the importance of prayer and spiritual growth. He therefore values it when God's people pray for him.

Dear God, I pray for our pastor today. Help and guide him in his important work and bless him with Your abundant blessings. Amen.

Prayerless Christians

Pray for us, too, that God may open a door
for our message, so that we may proclaim the
mystery of Christ, for which I am in chains.
Pray that I may proclaim it clearly, as I should.
Colossians 4:3-4

The more holy a person is, the more he values prayer; the clearer he sees that God gives Himself to praying people. The Holy Spirit never abides in a spirit that does not pray. Christ knows nothing of prayerless Christians.

Gifts, talents, education, eloquence, and God's call cannot lessen the demand of prayer, but only intensify the necessity for the preacher to pray and to be prayed for. And, if he is a true preacher, he will feel the necessity of prayer even more strongly.

He will not only feel the increasing demand to pray himself, but to call on others to help him through their prayers.

Father, I pray for preachers around the world today; that You will open the doors for their message as they tell the world of Your love for us. Amen.

The Church Equals Its Leaders

Stand firm in all the will of God,
mature and fully assured.
Colossians 4:12

Preachers are pre-eminently God's leaders. They are primarily responsible for the condition of the Church. They shape its character and give tone and direction to its life. Much depends on these leaders. They shape the times and the institutions.

The Church is divine; the treasure it holds is heavenly. But it bears the imprint of the human. The treasure is in earthen vessels. The Church of God makes, or is made by its leaders.

The Church will be what its leaders are: spiritual if they are so; worldly if they are; conglomerate if its leaders are.

God, I pray for the leaders in my church today and the important work they do. Bless them, Lord, but lead them also to lead us to be more like You. Amen.

July 23

A Pulpit without Prayer

*Know this love that surpasses knowledge – that you
may be filled to the measure of all the fullness of God.*
Ephesians 3:19

Strong spiritual leaders – people of holy might – are tokens of God's favor. Times of spiritual leadership are times of great spiritual prosperity to the church. Prayer is one of the eminent characteristics of strong spiritual leadership.

People of mighty prayer are people of power, and they shape the outcome of things. How can a person who does not get his message fresh from God in prayer expect to preach? A preacher's lips must be touched by the burning flame of prayer.

As far as the real interests of Christianity are concerned, a pulpit without prayer will always be a barren thing.

*Almighty God, fill me and fill our spiritual leaders
with the measure of all the fullness of You. Amen.*

Paul, the Preacher

Pray in the Spirit on all occasions with all kinds of prayers and requests. With this in mind, be alert and always keep on praying for all the saints. Pray also for me, that whenever I open my mouth, words may be given me so that I will fearlessly make known the mystery of the gospel.
Ephesians 6:18-19

A preacher may preach in an official, or learned way, without really praying. But there is an immeasurable distance between this kind of preaching and the sowing of God's precious seed with holy hands and prayerful hearts. Paul is an illustration of this.

Paul exemplifies the fact that the preacher must be a man given to prayer. Paul pre-eminently demonstrates that the true apostolic preacher must have the prayers of other good people to give to his ministry its full quota of success.

Dear God, I pray for our pastor and all preachers that whenever they open their mouths, You will give them words that will make the mystery of the gospel known. Amen.

July 25

Time with God

Is any one of you in trouble? He should pray.
Is anyone happy? Let him sing songs of praise.
James 5:13

Our devotional time is not measured by the clock, but time is of the essence. The ability to stay and wait essentially belongs to our fellowship with God.

Haste is often a part of the great business of communion with God. Short devotional time is the ruin of deep piety. Calmness, and strength are never the companions of haste. Short devotional time drains spiritual vigor and the root and bloom of the spiritual life.

Short devotional time is the number one reason for backsliding. It is a sure indication of superficial piety.

Forgive me, Father, for not always making enough time for You. I want to stay and wait in Your presence so that I can hear Your voice. Amen.

Praying Costs Time

You help us by your prayers.
2 Corinthians 1:11

Spiritual work is taxing work. Praying requires attention and time, which flesh and blood do not enjoy. Few people devote their time to prayer when earthly duty calls.

We sometimes become lax in our praying, and do not realize the peril until the damage has been done. Hasty devotions make weak faith, feeble convictions, and questionable piety.

To be little with God is to be little for God. To cut the praying short makes the whole Christian character short, miserable and careless.

Dear Lord God, help me not to become lax in my prayers. I want to spend more time with You, so that I can do more for You. Amen.

God's Full Flow

Pray for us that the message of the Lord
may spread rapidly and be honored,
just as it was with you. And pray that we might
be delivered from wicked and evil men.
2 Thessalonians 3:1-2

It takes time for the fullness of God to flow into the spirit. Short devotions cut the pipe of God's full flow. It takes time spent in earnest prayer to receive the full revelation of God. Little time and hurry spoil the picture.

More time and early hours devoted to prayer would revive and invigorate many a dead spiritual life.

More time and early hours for prayer would result in holy living. A holy life would not be so rare or so difficult if our devotions were not so short and hurried.

God, I know that more time spent with You will revive and invigorate my spiritual life. Please help me to set my priorities straight. You are the most important thing in my life. Amen.

Lingering in God's Presence

*"Will not God bring about justice for His
chosen ones, who cry out to Him day and night?"*
Luke 18:7

A Christly temper would not be such a foreign thing
if our prayer lives were intensified. We are sometimes miserable because we do not pray enough.

Time spent with God will bring abundance to our
lives. When we are devoted to God in our personal
quiet time, we will be devoted to Him in public.

Hasty prayers are without results. Lingering in
God's presence instructs and wins. We are taught
by it, and the greatest victories are often the results
of great waiting – waiting until words and plans
are exhausted. Silent and patient waiting gains the
crown.

*Father God, I want to linger in the Your presence.
I want to cry out to You day and night. Please guide
me. Amen.*

July 29

Prepared Hearts

Finally, brothers, pray for us that the message
of the Lord may spread rapidly and be honored.
2 Thessalonians 3:1

Prayer means the success of the preaching of the Word. It creates an atmosphere that is favorable for the Word to accomplish its purpose.

The parable of the sower is a notable study of preaching, showing its differing effects and describing the diversity of hearers. The wayside hearers are many. The soil lies unprepared. As a consequence, the devil easily takes away the seed (which is the Word of God).

If only the hearers would prepare the ground of their hearts beforehand by prayer and meditation, much of the current sowing would be fruitful.

Dear Lord God, help us to prepare the ground better through our prayers, so that Your Word will take root in people's hearts and produce a crop. Amen.

Cultivated Hearts

"Therefore consider carefully how you listen."
Luke 8:18

The parable of the sower shows us the different responses of the stony-ground and thorny-ground hearers. Although the Word lodges in their hearts and begins to sprout, all is lost, mainly because there is no cultivation afterwards.

The good-ground hearers are profited by the sowing, simply because their minds have been prepared for the reception of the seed. After hearing, they have cultivated the seed sown in their hearts by the exercise of prayer.

All this emphasizes the conclusion of this striking parable: In order to carefully consider how we hear, we must give ourselves continually to prayer.

Dear God, I want to hear Your Word and understand it, I want Your message to fall on good soil so that it may yield a crop for Your glory. Amen.

July 31

August

Conduct:
the Offspring of Character

Be self-controlled and alert. Your enemy the devil prowls around like a roaring lion looking for someone to devour.
1 Peter 5:8

It is true that prayer governs conduct, and conduct shapes character. Conduct is what we do. Character is what we are. Conduct is the outward life. Character is the unseen life, hidden within, yet is evidenced by what is seen. Conduct is external, seen from without. Character is internal, operating within.

In the economy of grace, conduct is the offspring of character. Character is the state of the heart and conduct is its outward expression. Prayer is related to all the gifts of grace.

Prayer helps to establish character and to shape conduct. And both depend on prayer for their successful continuance.

Father, I know that the successful continuance of how I act and who I am depend on prayer. Please guide me in Your truth today. Amen.

August 1

The True Test of Consecration

If My people, who are called by My name, will humble themselves and pray and seek My face and turn from their wicked ways, then will I hear from heaven and will forgive their sin and will heal their land.
2 Chronicles 7:14

There is much talk today of consecration, and many are considered consecrated people. A lot of these people; however, do not grasp the true meaning of this word.

The central trouble with all this false consecration is that there is no prayer in it. Here is the true test of consecration: it is a life of prayer. Unless prayer is in the forefront, the consecration is faulty, deceptive, falsely named.

Does he pray? That is the test of every so-called consecrated person. Is he a person of prayer? No consecration is worth a thought if it is devoid of prayer, and primarily a life of prayer.

I humble myself before You, Lord. I pray and seek Your face. Please hear my cries to You. Amen.

August 2

Inward Spiritual Character

[Jesus Christ] who gave Himself for us to redeem us
from all wickedness and to purify for Himself a people
that are His very own, eager to do what is good.
Titus 2:14

There may be a certain degree of moral character and conduct independent of prayer, but there cannot be any distinctive religious character and Christian conduct without it. Prayer helps where all other aids fail. We become better people and we live purer lives through constant prayer.

The very end and purpose of the atoning work of Christ is to create religious character and practice Christian conduct.

In Christ's teaching, it is not simply works of charity and deeds of mercy that He insists upon, but inward spiritual character. This much is demanded, and nothing short of it will be enough.

Dear God, You teach us that You do not simply require good deeds. You require an inward spiritual character which is developed by constant prayer. Amen.

August 3

God's Factory on Earth

*For it is God who works in you to will
and to act according to His good purpose.*
Philippians 2:13

The purpose of prayer is to change the character and conduct of people. In countless instances, change has been brought about by prayer. The church is presumed to be righteous and should be engaged in turning people to righteousness.

The church is God's factory on earth. Its primary duty is to create and foster righteous character. This is its very highest aim. Primarily, its work is not to acquire members or accumulate numbers. Its aim is not to get money or engage in deeds of charity and works of mercy.

Its work is to produce righteousness of character and purity of the outward life.

Almighty God, guide and direct our church in turning people to righteousness so that Your name may be glorified on earth through our works. Amen.

The Human Side of Holiness

If you fully obey the LORD your God and carefully follow all His commands I give you today, the LORD your God will set you high above all the nations on earth.
Deuteronomy 28:1

Consecration is not all there is to holiness. Many make serious mistakes at this point. Consecration makes us relatively holy. Our lives become more holy when we live closer to God.

Consecration is the human side of holiness. In this sense, it is self-sanctification. But sanctification, or holiness in its truest and highest sense, is divine, the act of the Holy Spirit working in the heart, making it clean, and putting therein a higher degree of the fruit of the Spirit.

Lord God, lead me by the help of Your Holy Spirit to fully obey and follow Your commands so that my life can produce the best fruit. Amen.

August 5

Products of Prayer

We demolish arguments and every pretension that sets itself up against the knowledge of God, and we take captive every thought to make it obedient to Christ.
2 Corinthians 10:5

A product reflects and partakes of the character of the manufacturer that makes it. A righteous church with a righteous purpose makes righteous people.

Prayer produces cleanliness of heart and purity of life. It can produce nothing else. Unrighteous behavior is born in the absence of prayer. The two go hand in hand. Prayer and sinning cannot keep company with each other. One or the other must stop.

Get people to pray, and they will stop sinning, because prayer creates a distaste for sinning. It lifts the entire nature to a reverent contemplation of high and holy things.

God, I want to pray more often. I want to pray always so that cleanliness and purity of heart will be evident in my life. Amen.

Praying in Color

*You will keep in perfect peace him whose mind
is steadfast, because he trusts in You.*
Isaiah 26:3

Prayer is based on character. What we are with God determines our influence with Him.

It was the inner character, not the outward appearance of men like Abraham, Job, David, Moses and others, that had such great influence with God in the biblical days. Today, it is not so much our words, but what we really are that counts with God. Conduct affects character and counts for much in our praying.

At the same time, character affects conduct to a far greater extent and has a superior influence over prayer. Our inner lives give color to our praying.

Dear Father, who we really are inside is what matters to You. I pray again today for You to create a pure heart within me and to renew my spirit. Amen.

A Life of Personal Holiness

*Let us draw near to God with a sincere heart
in full assurance of faith, having our hearts
sprinkled to cleanse us from a guilty conscience
and having our bodies washed with pure water.*
Hebrews 10:22

Consecration is much more than a life of so-called service. It is a life of personal holiness. It is that which brings spiritual power into the heart and brightens up the entire inner man. It is a life that always recognizes God, and a life given up to true prayer.

Full consecration is the highest type of Christian life. It is the one thing for which the believer should aim. He should never be satisfied until he is fully, entirely the Lord's by his own consent. His praying naturally and involuntarily leads up to this one act.

Dear Father God, I desire to live a life of full consecration to You. This is my aim. Please help and guide me. Amen.

Praying by Your Life

"Be careful or your hearts will be weighed down with dissipation, drunkenness and the anxieties of life, and that day will close on you unexpectedly like a trap.
Luke 21:34

Christian experience often collapses on the rock of conduct. It is the life that counts. Our praying suffers, like other phases of our religious experience, because of bad living.

In early times, preachers were ordered to preach by their lives or not preach at all. Christians everywhere ought to be reminded to pray by their lives or not pray at all. The best preaching, even in the pulpit, is that which is strengthened by the preacher living a godly life.

The most effective work done by people in the pews is accompanied by holiness of life. People preach by their lives, not by their words.

Lord, I want to mirror You to the world through my actions, so that others will believe in You without me having to say a word. Amen.

August 9

Prayer of Repentance

If anyone is in Christ, he is a new creation;
the old has gone, the new has come!
2 Corinthians 5:17

The prayer of repentance is surely acceptable to God. He delights in hearing the cries of remorseful sinners. But repentance involves not only sorrow for sin, but turning away from wrongdoing and learning to do good. True repentance produces a change in character and behavior.

We have missed the whole purpose of prayer if it fails to shape our character and correct our behavior. Cold, formal praying may exist side by side with bad behavior, but such praying is no praying at all. Our praying advances in power just as much as it rectifies the life. A prayerful life will grow in purity and devotion to God.

Dear God, I confess my sins and lay them before You today. Please forgive me and guide me through Your Spirit so that I can turn away from wrong, and do right instead. Amen.

August 10

A Brass Door

Therefore confess your sins to each other and
pray for each other so that you may be healed.
The prayer of a righteous man is powerful and effective.
James 5:16

The character of the inner life is a condition of effective praying. As the life is, so the praying will be.

The prayer of the righteous always achieves much. Indeed, one may go further and say that it is only the prayer of the righteous that achieves anything at all.

The oppression of our lives often breaks the force of our praying and is like a brass door in the face of prayer.

To have your eyes on God's glory and to be possessed by an earnest desire to please Him in all your ways give power to prayer.

Father God, clean my life from all wrongdoing. I want my life to be pleasing to You. Amen.

August 11

The Fruit of Real Prayer

Be wise about what is good,
and innocent about what is evil.
Romans 16:19

Praying must come out of a clean heart. It must be strengthened by a life striving to obey God.

Let us not forget that, while life is a condition of prayer, prayer is also the condition of righteous living. The fruit of real praying is right living. It causes a person to watch his temper, conversation, and conduct. It leads him to walk cautiously and redeem the time. It enables him to act worthy of being a Christian.

It gives him a high incentive to pursue his pilgrimage consistently by shunning every evil way to walk in the light of God.

Dear Lord God, I know that if I want my prayers to be real, I must live right. Help me to be excellent about what is good, and innocent of evil. Amen.

The Multi-Sidedness of Prayer

His divine power has given us everything we need
for life and godliness through our knowledge of
Him who called us by His own glory and goodness.
2 Peter 1:3

When we study the multi-sidedness of prayer, we may be surprised at the number of things with which it is connected.

Consecration is one of the things to which prayer is closely related. Prayer leads up to and governs consecration. Much goes under the name of consecration that has no consecration in it. Popular consecration is sadly at fault because it has little or no prayer in it.

Consecration that has not resulted from living a life of prayer is not consecration. Prayer is the one prominent thing in a consecrated life.

Father, I know that all that I need for a consecrated life
is to pray and to know more of You every day. Amen.

August 13

Marvelous Change

He saved us, not because of righteous things
we had done, but because of His mercy.
Titus 3:5

The Christian religion deals with people who are lacking spiritual character and who live unholy lives. It aims to change them so that they can become holy in heart and righteous in life.

This is where prayer enters and demonstrates its wonderful ability and fruit. Prayer drives one toward this specific end. In fact, without prayer, no change in moral character is ever possible. This marvelous change is brought to pass through earnest, persistent, faithful prayer.

Any assumed form of Christianity that does not cause this change in the hearts of people is a delusion and a snare.

Dear Lord, I want to thank You and praise You for the mercy and grace You show me. Amen.

Complete Surrender

*Whatever was to my profit I now consider loss
for the sake of Christ. What is more, I consider everything
a loss compared to the surpassing greatness of knowing
Christ Jesus my Lord, for whose sake I have lost all things.
I consider them rubbish, that I may gain Christ.*
Philippians 3:7-8

Consecration is the voluntary dedication of oneself to God. It is the setting apart of all we are, all we have, and all we expect to have or be. God must always come first.

It is not so much the giving of ourselves to the church. We must focus our eyes on God; He is the Source of all consecration. It is a separation of oneself to God, a devoting of all that He is and has to a sacred use.

Consecration has a sacred nature. It is devoted to holy ends. It is putting yourself willingly into God's hands to be used sacredly, with sanctifying ends in view.

I devote my life and all that I am to You today, Lord. I choose this day to serve You. Amen.

August 15

Separation for Holy Use

Let us draw near to God with a sincere heart
in full assurance of faith, having our hearts sprinkled
to cleanse us from a guilty conscience and
having our bodies washed with pure water.
Hebrews 10:22

Consecration is much more than setting oneself apart from sinful things. It is living a holy life as opposed to a worldly life. It is living a life that is devoted to God and His purpose for you. It is devoting all we have to God for His use.

The consecration that meets God's demands is a complete consecration, with no mental reservation. To make a half-hearted, partial consecration is to make no consecration at all.

It involves our whole being, all we have and all that we are. Everything is definitely and willingly placed in God's hands for His supreme use.

I place all that I am in Your hands, God. I want my life to be fully set apart for Your plans and purposes. Amen.

August 16

Bad Praying = Bad Living

*When you spread out your hands in prayer, I will
hide My eyes from you; even if you offer many prayers,
I will not listen. Your hands are full of blood.*
Isaiah 1:15

Bad living means bad praying and, in the end, no
praying at all. The stream of prayer cannot rise
higher than the fountain of living.

We simply cannot talk strongly, intimately and
confidently to God unless we are faithfully and truly living for Him. Our quiet time before God cannot
become sanctified if our lives are not familiar with
His laws and purposes.

We must learn this lesson well. Righteous character and Christlike conduct give us a peculiar and
favored standing in prayer before God.

The Word places special emphasis on the part that
our behavior plays on the value of our prayers.

*Father, I know that successful prayer goes hand in
hand with a life that pleases You. See if there is any offensive way in me, and lead me in the way everlasting.
Amen.*

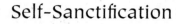

Self-Sanctification

*"Consecrate yourselves and be holy, because
I am the Lord your God. Keep My decrees and
follow them. I am the Lord, who makes you holy."*
Leviticus 20:7-8

Here we are told to sanctify ourselves, and then in the next sentence we are taught that it is the Lord who sanctifies us.

Here is the two-fold meaning of sanctification, and a distinction that you always need to keep in mind. God does not consecrate us to His service; we must wholeheartedly commit or consecrate ourselves to Him. But we do not sanctify ourselves – it is the work of the Spirit in us.

Consecration is the intentional act of the believer and is the direct result of prayer. No prayerless person can ever understand the idea of full consecration.

I commit myself to You, God. Sanctify me through the work of Your indwelling Spirit. I cannot do this on my own. Amen.

Praying Shapes Consecrated People

"Do you not know that your body is a temple of the Holy Spirit, who is in you, whom you have received from God? You are not your own; you were bought at a price."
1 Corinthians 6:19-20

A life without prayer and consecration have nothing in common. A life of prayer naturally leads to full consecration. Consecration fully recognizes God's ownership of us. Praying shapes consecrated people.

As prayer leads up to and brings forth full consecration, so prayer entirely influences a consecrated life. The prayer life and the consecrated life are intimate companions. They are Siamese twins, inseparable. Prayer enters into every phase of a consecrated life. A life without prayer that claims consecration is false.

Thank You, God, for the gift of prayer and that our prayers offered to You can produce a consecrated life. Amen.

August 19

On Praying Ground

"No one can serve two masters. Either he will hate the one and love the other, or he will be devoted to the one and despise the other. You cannot serve both God and Money."
Matthew 6:24

Consecration is really devoting oneself to a life of prayer. It means not only to pray, but to pray consistently and effectively.

God cannot deny the requests of the man who has completely dedicated himself to God and His service. This act of the consecrated man puts him on praying ground and pleading terms with God.

It puts Him in reach of God. It places him where he can get hold of God, and where he can influence God to do things that He would not otherwise do.

Thank You, Almighty God, that our prayers can move You. I devote myself to You today. Amen.

Complete Surrender

*When you ask, you do not receive, because
you ask with wrong motives, that you may
spend what you get on your pleasures.*
James 4:3

God can depend on consecrated people. God can afford to commit Himself to those who have fully committed themselves to Him in prayer. He who gives all to God will get all from God.

As prayer is the condition of full consecration, so prayer is the habit, the rule, of him who has dedicated himself wholly to God. Prayer is the most appropriate thing in the consecrated life.

Prayer is part of the consecrated life. Prayer is the constant, the inseparable, the intimate companion of consecration. They walk and talk together.

Dear Father God, thank You that I can know that if I give my all to You, I will get all from You. Amen.

Consecrated Service

To rescue us from the hand of our enemies,
and to enable us to serve Him without fear in
holiness and righteousness before Him all our days.
Luke 1:74-75

God wants consecrated followers because they can pray and will pray. He can use consecrated people because He can use praying people. Consecration and prayer meet in the same person.

Prayer is the tool with which the consecrated person works. The prime purpose of consecration is not service in the ordinary sense of the word. Consecration aims at the right sort of service, the scriptural kind.

It seeks to serve God, but in an entirely different way from that which is in the minds of church leaders and workers.

Dear God, I want to be a praying servant of You so that You can use me in Your service. I want to live holy and righteous before You. Amen.

Living Right

Do everything without complaining or arguing,
so that you may become blameless and pure,
children of God without fault in a crooked and
depraved generation, in which you shine like stars
in the universe as you hold out the Word of life.
Philippians 2:14-16

In the Epistles, the focus is not on church activities, but rather on the personal life.

It is good behavior, righteous conduct, godly conversation, holy living and a controlled temper – things that belong primarily to the personal life in religion.

Religion directs one to right living. Religion shows itself in life. In this way religion proves its reality, its sincerity and its divinity.

Father God, make me a shining star in Your universe so that I may boast on the day of Christ that I did not labor for nothing. But to receive the crown of glory and eternal life from You. Amen.

A Holy Life

But you are not to be like that. Instead, the
greatest among you should be like the youngest,
and the one who rules like the one who serves.
Luke 22:26

The first aim of consecration is holiness of heart and of life. It is to glorify God by a holy life flowing from a heart cleansed from all sin.

To cultivate this kind of life and heart, one must be watchful, one must pray and be forgiving toward others. A true Christian seeks holiness of heart, He is not satisfied without it.

For this very purpose he consecrates himself to God. He gives himself entirely over to God in order to be holy in heart and in life.

Holiness of heart and life satisfy You, God. Cleanse me from all unrighteousness for Your glory. Amen.

Consecration and Holiness

Commit your way to the LORD;
trust in Him and He will do this. He will make
your righteousness shine like the dawn.
Psalm 37:5-6

Holiness of heart is thoroughly inspired by prayer. It takes prayer to bring one into such a consecrated life of holiness to the Lord.

Holy people are praying people. Holiness of heart and life encourage people to pray. Those who are unfamiliar with praying in solitude are not at all interested in consecration and holiness. Holiness thrives in the place of secret prayer.

In solitary prayer, holiness is found. Consecration brings forth holiness of heart, and prayer stands by when this is done.

Almighty God, I commit all my ways to You so that You may lift me up in due time and make me holy like You are holy. Amen.

The Best Hours of the Day

*One of those days Jesus went out to a mountainside
to pray, and spent the night praying to God.*
Luke 6:12

To pray is the greatest thing we can do; and to do it
well there must be calmness, time, and deliberation.
Otherwise, it is degraded into something small and
insignificant.

We cannot do too much real praying. If we want
to learn the wondrous art, we must not offer a frag-
ment here and there – "A little talk with Jesus," as
the chorus goes. But we must demand and hold the
best hours of the day for God and prayer, or there
will be no praying worth the name.

*I want to give the best hours of every day to You, my
Lord and my God. Please help me to set my priorities
straight. Amen.*

The Lost Art of Prayer

Brothers, pray for us.
1 Thessalonians 5:25

In the hustle and bustle of life today people don't take time to pray. There are laymen who will give their money, but they will not give themselves to prayer.

There are plenty of preachers who will preach on the need of revival and the spread of the Kingdom of God. But there are many who will do that without prayer which makes all the preaching worthless.

To many people prayer is out of date; almost a lost art. The greatest benefactor that this age could have is the person who will bring the preachers and the church back to prayer.

In this busy age today, people have little time for anything. I want to make time for You, God, because I can't go one day without You. Amen.

August 27

The Spirit's Most Urgent Call

In the same way, the Spirit helps us in our weakness. We do not know what we ought to pray for, but the Spirit Himself intercedes for us with groans that words cannot express.
Romans 8:26

The apostles only grasped a little bit of the great importance of prayer before Pentecost. But the Spirit coming at Pentecost elevated prayer to its vital position in the gospel of Christ.

The call of prayer to every saint is the Spirit's most urgent call. Sainthood's piety is made and perfected by prayer. Where are the Christlike leaders who can teach the modern saints how to pray and put them at it?

An increase in educational facilities and a great increase in money will be the direct curse to Christianity if they are not sanctified by more and better praying than we are doing.

O God, I thank You for giving us Your Holy Spirit who helps us in our weaknesses. When we don't know what to pray, He prays for us. Amen.

Praying Leaders have Praying Followers

In all my prayers for all of you, I always pray with joy.
Philippians 1:4

Increased prayer will not happen as a matter of course. Only praying leaders can have praying followers.

Praying apostles will produce praying saints. We greatly need somebody who can set the saints to this business of praying. Who will restore this breach? He who can set the church to praying will be the greatest of reformers and apostles.

If this is realized, our prayers, faith, lives, and ministry will take on such a radical and aggressive form that it will bring about spiritual revival in people and in the church.

Father, thank You for praying leaders. Please guide the leaders in our church to bring people back to You and back to praying. Amen.

August 29

The World Turned Upside-Down

*"Ask the Lord of the harvest, therefore,
to send out workers into His harvest field."*
Matthew 9:38

God can work wonders if He has a suitable man.
People can work wonders if they let God lead them.
The full gift of the Spirit which turned the world
upside-down would be useful in these days.

People who can stir things mightily for God,
whose spiritual revolutions change the whole aspect of things, are the universal need of the church.

The church has never been without these people.
They are the standing miracles of the divinity of the
church. Their example and history are an unfailing
inspiration and blessing. We should pray that such
people would increase in number and power.

*I pray today, Father God, that men and women who
can stir things mightily for Your good purposes will increase in number and power in the world. Amen.*

August 30

Doing Great Things for God

*"I tell you the truth, anyone who has faith in Me
will do what I have been doing. He will do even greater
things than these, because I am going to the Father."*
John 14:12

The past has not exhausted the possibilities or the
demands of doing great things for God. The church
that is dependent on its past history for its miracles
of power and grace is a fallen church.

God wants people who look to Him with pure
hearts. People who are willing to sacrifice self and
the world in order to do God's will.

Let us pray that God's promises to prayer may
be more than realized.

*Dear God, I thank You that I can do great things
by believing in Your Word and holding on to Your promises. Amen.*

September

Faith in Action

*"Whoever has My commands and obeys
them, he is the one who loves Me."*
John 14:21

Unquestionably, obedience is a high virtue, the quality of a soldier. A soldier has to be obedient. This obedience must be without questioning or complaining. Obedience is faith in action. It is the outflow, the very test of love.

The gift of the Holy Spirit in full measure and in richer experience depends on loving obedience. Obedience to God is a condition of spiritual abundance, inward satisfaction and stability of heart.

Obedience opens the gates of the Holy City and gives access to the Tree of Life.

Dear heavenly Father, I want to be obedient to You with all my heart and soul. I know that obedience opens the gate for the gift of Your Holy Spirit. Amen.

September 1

Our Destination

Therefore let us leave the elementary teachings
about Christ and go on to maturity.
Hebrews 6:1

It is essential, in our Christian walk, that we have something definite in view and that we strike out for that one goal.

It is important that we do not lose sight of the starting point in a religious life, and that we measure the steps already walked.

But it is likewise necessary to keep the end in view and that the steps required to reach the standard are always in sight.

Dear God, my eyes are fixed on You, the Author and Perfecter of my faith. Please help me to never lose sight of You. Amen.

September 2

Keeping All the Commandments

"Oh, that their hearts would be inclined to fear Me and keep all My commands always, so that it might go well with them and their children forever."
Deuteronomy 5:29

The keeping of all God's commandments is the demonstration of the obedience that God requires from us. Can a believer receive help to obey every one of them? Of course. All that a person needs to do is pray.

Does God give commandments that we cannot obey? No. In all of Scripture, not a single instance is recorded of God having commanded any man to do a thing that was beyond his power.

Is God so inconsiderate to require of man something that he is unable to do? Certainly not. That is against God's character.

Dear Lord God, thank You that You will not let me be tempted beyond what I can bear. Amen.

Our Heavenly Parent

"If you, then, though you are evil, know how to give good gifts to your children, how much more will your Father in heaven give good gifts to those who ask Him!"
Matthew 7:11

Think about this thought for a moment. Do earthly parents require their children to perform duties that they cannot do? What father would be so unjust and mean? Are our earthly parents kinder, better, more just than our perfect God?

In principle, obedience to God is the same quality as obedience to earthly parents. It implies the giving up of one's own way to follow that of another. It implies the submission of oneself to the authority and requirements of a parent.

Loving Father, I submit myself to Your authority and give up my own ways to obey You. You are a perfect God, and deserve the best from us. Guide me in obedience today. Amen.

It Pays to Be Obedient

"You may ask Me for anything in My name, and I will do it. If you love Me, you will obey what I command."
John 14:14-15

Commands, either from our heavenly Father or our earthly father, are directed by love. All such commands are in the best interests of those who are commanded. God has issued His commands to us in order to make us prosper.

It pays, therefore, to be obedient. Obedience brings its own reward. God has made it so. Since He has, we can know that He would never ask us to do anything that we aren't capable of doing, or that we can't do.

Obedience is love fulfilling every command. It is love expressing itself.

Dear Father God, I know that You give us commands in order to make us prosper. Thank You, Lord, that I may know that You reward obedience. Amen.

September 5

At God's Disposal

Then there will be righteous sacrifices,
whole burnt offerings to delight You;
then bulls will be offered on Your altar.
Psalm 51:19

Prayer leads to full consecration. Consecration is but the silent expression of prayer. The prayer life is the direct fruit of entire consecration to God.

No consecration is pleasing to God that is not perfect in all its parts. Consecration is putting oneself entirely at the disposal of God. And God wants and commands all His consecrated ones to be praying people.

This is the one definite standard at which we must aim. We cannot afford to seek anything lower than this.

God, my aim today is to be fully consecrated to You. I surrender myself completely to You – use me for Your divine purposes. Amen.

Supplies of Grace

*The law is holy, and the commandment
is holy, righteous and good.*
Romans 7:12

It is really much easier to please God than to please people. Moreover, we can *know* when we please Him. This is the witness of the Spirit – the inward, divine assurance given to all the children of God that they are doing their Father's will and that their ways are well pleasing in His sight.

God's commandments, then, can be obeyed by all who seek supplies of grace to enable them to obey. These commandments must be obeyed. God's government is at stake.

The spirit of rebellion is the very essence of sin. It is the denial of God's authority that He cannot tolerate.

Heavenly Father I ask for Your grace to help me obey Your commands. Amen.

September 7

God's Enabling Act

For God did not give us a spirit of timidity,
but a spirit of power, of love and of self-discipline.
2 Timothy 1:7

If anyone complains that man under the Fall is too weak to obey, the answer is that, through the Atonement of Christ, man is able to obey.

The Atonement is God's enabling act. God works in us, through regeneration and the Holy Spirit, giving us grace that is sufficient. This grace is furnished without measure in answer to prayer.

So, while God commands, He stands pledged to give us all the necessary strength to meet His demands. Because this is true, man has no excuse for disobedience. He may serve the Lord with reverence and godly fear.

Dear God, because Christ died for us, and because You gave us Your Holy Spirit to comfort us, we are able to obey You and meet Your demands. Thank You, Father. Amen.

Partaker of the Divine Nature

"I desire to do Your will, O my God."
Psalm 40:8

Those who say it is impossible to keep God's commandments overlook one important consideration.

It is the vital truth that, through prayer and faith, man's nature is changed and made a partaker of the divine nature. The inability to keep God's commandments because of a weak, fallen state is removed.

By this radical change in moral nature, a believer receives power to obey God in every way. Because of this, rebellion is removed and is replaced by a heart that gladly obeys God's Word.

I desire to do Your will, O God. Thank You that through faith and prayer, we receive power and strength to obey. Amen.

Boldness Before the Throne

*Who may ascend the hill of the LORD? He who
has clean hands and a pure heart, who does not lift
up his soul to an idol or swear by what is false.*
Psalm 24:3-4

Obedience can ask with boldness at the throne of grace.

The disobedient person is timid in his approach and hesitant in his supplication. Such a person is stopped by his wrongdoing. The requesting, obedient child comes into the presence of his Father with confidence and boldness. Obedience frees one from the dread of acting disobediently and instead, gives courage.

To do God's will without hesitation is the joy and the privilege of the successful praying man. He who has clean hands and a pure heart can pray with confidence.

Father, I want to experience the joy and privilege of successful praying by doing Your will without hesitation. Guide me through Your Spirit. Amen.

The Christian's Trade

Search me, O God, and know my heart; test me
and know my anxious thoughts. See if there is any
offensive way in me, and lead me in the way everlasting.
Psalm 139:23-24

"The Christian's trade," said Martin Luther, "is prayer." But the Christian has another trade to learn before he proceeds to learn the secrets of the trade of prayer. He must learn perfect obedience to the Father's will. Obedience follows love, and prayer follows obedience.

One who has been disobedient may pray. A person may come to God's feet with tears, confession, and a heart full of regret.

God will hear him and answer his prayer.

God, I want to obey You. Search me, O God, and know my heart. Lead me in the way everlasting. Amen.

An Obedient Life

*If our hearts do not condemn us, we have confidence
before God and receive from Him everything we ask,
because we obey His commands and do what pleases Him.*
1 John 3:21-22

A life of obedience helps prayer. It speeds prayer to the throne. God cannot help hearing the prayer of an obedient child. Unquestioning obedience counts much in the sight of God at the throne of heavenly grace.

It acts like the flowing tides of many rivers. An obedient life is not simply a reformed life. It is not the old life primed and repainted. It is not a superficial churchgoing life or a flurry of activities.

Neither is it only an external conformation to what society expects. It takes much more than this to be a truly obedient Christian.

Dear Lord God, I know that it pleases You when we are obedient to You. Please guide me so that I may hear Your voice more clearly. Amen.

Free Access to God

May God Himself, the God of peace, sanctify you through
and through. May your whole spirit, soul and body
be kept blameless at the coming of our Lord Jesus Christ.
1 Thessalonians 5:23

A life of full obedience, a life that is focused on God, will not be distracted by any obstacles while praying.

If you have an earnest desire to pray well, you must learn to obey well. If you have a desire to learn to pray, then you must have an earnest desire to learn how to do God's will.

If you want to have free access to God in prayer, then every obstacle in the nature of sin or disobedience must be removed.

God delights in the prayers of obedient children.

Through obedience to You, Father God, we can ask for anything in Your name, and You will do it. I praise Your holy name. Amen.

Baptizing Tears

In the same way, the Spirit helps us in our weakness. We do not know what we ought to pray for, but the Spirit Himself intercedes for us with groans that words cannot express.
Romans 8:26

Requests coming from the lips of those who delight to do God's will, reach His ears with great speed. God answers them promptly.

In themselves, tears are not rewarding. Yet, they have their uses in prayer. Tears should baptize our place of supplication. The person who has never wept over his sins has never really prayed. Tears, sometimes, are a prodigal's only plea. But tears are for the past; for sin and wrongdoing.

There is another step and stage waiting to be taken. That step is unquestioning obedience. Until it is taken, prayer for blessing and continued sustenance will be of no use.

Dear heavenly Father, I come before You in earnest prayer and ask You to please forgive my sins and have mercy on me. Thank You for Your Holy Spirit that intercedes for us in prayer. Amen.

Shaping Character

*The LORD detests men of perverse heart but
He delights in those whose ways are blameless.*
Proverbs 11:20

Much of the feebleness of religion results from the
failure to have a scriptural standard in religion by
which to shape character. This largely results from
the omission of prayer or the failure to emphasize
the importance of prayer.

We cannot determine our spiritual growth if we
have nothing to measure it against. There must always be something definite before the mind's eye at
which we are aiming and to which we are driving.

Neither can there be inspiration if there is nothing greater to stimulate us.

*Father God, let my only aim be to become more and
more like Jesus every day. Amen.*

The Sweetest Experience

Be joyful always; pray continually; give thanks in all circumstances, for this is God's will for you in Christ Jesus.
1 Thessalonians 5:16-18

Many Christians are without purpose because they have nothing on which to shape their conduct and character.

There is nothing to keep them focused, determined and on the right path. Prayer helps one gain a clearer, more focused idea of religion.

In fact, prayer itself is a very definite thing; it aims at something specific, it has a mark at which it aims. Prayer aims at the most definite, the highest, and the sweetest religious experience.

Thank You, God, for giving us Your Word upon which we can shape our lives. Lord, You give purpose and meaning to our lives. Amen.

Wanting All of God

*I thank God, whom I serve, as my forefathers
did, with a clear conscience, as night and
day I constantly remember you in my prayers.*
2 Timothy 1:3

Praying people want all that God has in store for them. They are not satisfied with a low religious life; superficial, vague, and indefinite.

Praying people constantly strive for more. They are not after being saved from some sin, but saved from all sin, both inward and outward.

They are not only after deliverance from sinning, but from sin itself, from its being, its power, and its pollution. They are after holiness of heart and life.

Dear Lord God, I want to receive all that You have in store for me. Please help me to pray without ceasing. Amen.

The Standard of a Religious Life

*What is more, I consider everything a loss compared
to the surpassing greatness of knowing Christ
Jesus my Lord, for whose sake I have lost all things.
I consider them rubbish, that I may gain Christ.*
Philippians 3:8

Prayer believes in and seeks for the very highest religious life set before us in the Word of God. When we make our own standards, there is delusion and falsity for our desires, convenience and pleasure form the rule, and that is always a fleshly and a low rule.

From it, all the fundamental principles of a Christ-centered religion are left out. When we allow others to set our standard of religion, it is generally deficient because, valuable virtues may be lost, whilst defects are carried through.

God, I pray for Your help in setting my standard of religion. I consider all things a loss, that I may gain Christ. Amen.

September 18

Religious Opinions

*He gave Himself for us to redeem us from all
wickedness and to purify for Himself a people that
are His very own, eager to do what is good.*
Titus 2:14

The most serious damage in determining what religion is according to what others say, is in allowing current opinion to shape our religious character.

Commonplace religion is pleasing to flesh and blood. There is no self-denial in it. It is good enough for our neighbors. Others are living on a low plane, on a compromising level, living as the world lives. Why should we be different – striving for good works? But, are the easy-going crowds who are living prayerless lives going to heaven?

Is heaven a fit place for non-praying, ease-loving people? That is the supreme question.

*Dear Lord Jesus, You are the Way and the Truth and
the Life – the way to heaven. Amen.*

The Divine Rule

We, however, will not boast beyond proper limits,
but will continue our boasting to the field God
has assigned to us, a field that reaches even to you.
2 Corinthians 10:13

No standard of religion is worth a moment's consideration when it neglects prayer. No standard is worth any thought that does not make prayer the main thing in religion. A life of prayer is the divine rule.

This is the pattern, just as our Lord is the one Example that we must follow. Prayer is required for a spiritual life. It is God's standard at which we are aiming, not man's.

Our goal should be set not by the opinions of people, not by what they say, but by what the Scriptures say.

Father, I know that the divine rule is to live a life of prayer and obedience before You. I press on to reach the goal for which You have called me. Amen.

Full Consecration

Offer your bodies as living sacrifices,
holy and pleasing to God.
Romans 12:1

A low standard of religion lives by a low standard of praying.

Everything in our religious lives depends upon being definite. The definiteness of our religious experiences and of our living will depend on the definiteness of our views of what religion is and of the things of which it consists. There is only one way to be fully consecrated to God.

A full renunciation of self, and a sincere offering of all to God – this is the divine requirement. There is nothing vague in that. Nothing in that is governed by the opinions of others or affected by how people live around us.

Dear God, I surrender my life to You completely. I want to live a holy and pleasing life in Your sight. Please guide me. Amen.

September 21

Obeying Because of Love

*Receive from Him anything we ask, because
we obey His commands and do what pleases Him.*
1 John 3:22

Love delights to obey and please whom it loves. There are no hardships in love.

There may be demands, but no irritations. This is obedience, running ahead of every command. It is love, obeying by anticipation.

Those who say that men are bound to commit sin because of environment, heredity, or tendency are very wrong. Far be it from our heavenly Father to demand impossibilities of His children. It is possible to please Him in all things, for He is not hard to please.

Thank God it is possible for every child of God to please our heavenly Father!

Thank You, Lord, for not expecting the impossible from us. I know that I can do all things through You who gives me strength. Amen.

Experiencing Religion

My dear friends, as you have always obeyed –
not only in my presence, but now much more in my
absence – continue to work out your salvation with
fear and trembling, for it is God who works in you
to will and to act according to His good purpose.
Philippians 2:12-13

A scriptural standard of religion includes a clear religious experience. Religion involves experience. The new birth is a definite Christian experience.

The witness of the Spirit is not a vague *something*, but an inward assurance given by the Holy Spirit that we are the children of God. In fact, everything belonging to religious experience is clear, bringing conscious joy, peace and love.

This is the divine standard of religion, a standard attained by constant prayer and a religious experience kept alive and enlarged by the same means of prayer.

I thank You, God, for the inward assurance given by Your Holy Spirit that I am Your child. Amen.

Doing God's Will

*For whoever keeps the whole law and yet stumbles
at just one point is guilty of breaking all of it.*
James 2:10

What is obedience? It is doing God's will. How many of the commandments require obedience? To keep half of them and break the other half – is that real obedience? To keep all the commandments but one – is that obedience?

The spirit that prompts a man to break one commandment is the spirit that may move him to break them all. God's commandments are a unit. To break one strikes at the principle that underlies and runs through the whole.

He who does not hesitate to break a single commandment probably would, under the same stress and surrounded by the same circumstances, break them all.

Lord God, I know that by the help of Your indwelling Spirit, it is possible to obey Your laws. You are worthy of our praise. Amen.

Prayer Generates Love

*For you have been born again, not
of perishable seed, but of imperishable,
through the living and enduring word of God.*
1 Peter 1:23

Prayer invariably generates a love for the Word of God. Prayer leads people to obey the Word of God and puts an unspeakable joy into the obedient heart.

Praying people and Bible-reading people are the same kind of people. The God of the Bible and the God of prayer are one. God speaks to man in the Bible; man speaks to God in prayer. One reads the Bible to discover God's will and prays in order to receive power to do that will.

Bible reading and praying are the distinguishing traits of those who strive to know and please God.

Dear God, guide me in my prayers to You and in my Bible reading so that I may discover Your will. Amen.

September 25

A Church-Supporting Spirit

*Let us not give up meeting together,
as some are in the habit of doing.*
Hebrews 10:25

Just as prayer generates a love for the Scriptures and causes people to begin to read the Bible, so does prayer also cause men and women to visit the house of God to hear the Scriptures explained.

Churchgoing is closely connected with the Bible, primarily because the Bible cautions us against not giving up meeting together. Churchgoing also results because God's chosen minister explains and enforces the Scriptures upon his hearers. Prayer develops a resolve in those who practice it to not forsake the church.

Prayer generates a churchgoing conscience, a church-loving heart, and a church-supporting spirit. Praying people take delight in the preaching of the Word and the support of the church.

Father, help us not to give up meeting together and praying together with other believers. Amen.

Protection Against Sinning

I have hidden Your word in my heart
that I might not sin against You.
Psalm 119:11

Psalm 119 is a directory of God's Word. With three or four exceptions, each verse contains a word that identifies or locates the Word of God. Quite often, the psalmist knelt in supplication, praying several times.

Here, in verse 11, the psalmist found his protection against sin – by having God's Word hidden in his heart and his whole being filled with that Word.

We find that the power of prayer creates a real love for the Scriptures and puts within people a nature that will take pleasure in the Word.

Heavenly Father, by having Your Word hidden in my heart I know that I can be protected from doing wrong. Amen.

Jesus, a Man of Prayer

He went to Nazareth, where He had been brought up, and on the Sabbath day He went into the Synagogue, as was His custom.
Luke 4:16

Do we relish God's Word? If so, then let us give ourselves continually to prayer.

He who would have a heart for the reading of the Bible must not – dare not – forget to pray. A person who loves the Bible will also love to pray. A person who loves to pray will delight in the law of the Lord.

Our Lord was a man of prayer. He magnified the Word of God and often quoted the Scriptures. Right through His earthly life, Jesus observed Sabbath keeping, churchgoing, and the reading of the Word of God. His prayer intermingled with them all.

Dear Father, I give myself continually to You in prayer. Make me more and more like Jesus every day. Amen.

A Secret Place

*"When you pray, go into your room, close the door
and pray to your Father, who is unseen. Then your Father,
who sees what is done in secret, will reward you."*
Matthew 6:6

Let it be said that no two things are more essential to a Spirit-filled life than Bible reading and prayer.

They will help you to grow in grace, to obtain joy from living a Christian life, and to be established in the way of eternal peace. Neglecting these things paves the way for a life without purpose.

Reading God's Word regularly and praying habitually in a secret place of the Most High, puts one where one is absolutely safe from the attacks of the Enemy of souls. It guarantees a person salvation and final victory through the overcoming power of the Lamb.

God, thank You that I can live a life of victory because You have already overcome the world. Amen.

September 29

Fullness and Boldness

"Stay in the city until you have
been clothed with power from on high."
Luke 24:49

Without question the early church received the Lord's teaching that prayer is answered.

The certainty of the answer to prayer was as fixed as God's Word is true. The Holy Spirit came because the disciples put their faith into practice. They waited in the Upper Room in prayer for ten days, and the promise was fulfilled. The answer came just as Jesus said.

The answer to prayer was a response to their faith and prayer. The fullness of the Spirit always brings patience and boldness.

Thank You, Loving Father, that You always know best what we need. Thank You for giving us Your Holy Spirit. Amen.

September 30

October

Holy Praying

The smoke of the incense, together with the prayers of
the saints, went up before God from the angel's hand.
Revelation 8:4

It is important to understand that the praying that is given such a position as explained in Revelation, and from which great results flow, is not simply the saying of prayers, but holy praying.

Behind such praying, giving to it energy and flame, are men and women who are whole-heartedly devoted to God. They are entirely separated from sin and fully separated to God. They always give energy, force and strength to praying.

Our Lord Jesus Christ excelled in prayer because He was supreme in holiness.

Full surrender opens the door to the throne of grace. It influences God greatly.

Dear heavenly Father, please guide me through Your
Spirit so that my prayers will not be mere words ut-
tered, but holy praying. Amen.

Compassion for Others

The LORD is gracious and compassionate,
slow to anger and rich in love.
Psalm 145:8

Compassion develops and grows when a person is confronted by the deep needs and distress of people who are unable to help themselves. Helplessness appeals to compassion.

Compassion is silent, but does not remain secluded. It reaches out at the sight of trouble, sin and need.

First of all, compassion flows out in earnest prayer for those in need and has sympathy for them. Prayer for others is born of a sympathetic heart.

Prayer is natural and almost spontaneous when compassion grows in the heart. Prayer belongs to the compassionate believer.

Dear God, please grant me a compassionate and sympathetic heart for people. I want my prayers for others to flow from a heart overflowing with compassion. Amen.

October 2

The School of Suffering

*"You may ask Me for anything
in My name, and I will do it."*
John 14:14

Loving obedience moves us into the prayer realm. It makes us co-heirs of the wealth of Christ. We receive the riches of His grace through the Holy Spirit, who will abide with us and be in us. Obedience to God qualifies us to pray effectively.

Jesus learned obedience through suffering. At the same time, He learned prayer through obedience. Just as it is the prayer of a righteous person that avails much, so it is righteousness that is obedient to God.

A righteous person is an obedient person. He can accomplish great things when he goes to his knees.

Almighty God, I know that the prayer of a righteous man is powerful and effective. But I also know that righteousness means obeying You. Please help me be obedient. I want to glorify You with my life. Amen.

A Plentiful Harvest

"The harvest is plentiful but the workers are few.
Ask the Lord of the harvest, therefore,
to send out workers into His harvest field."
Matthew 9:37-38

We read in Scripture that our Lord had called His disciples aside to rest awhile, exhausted by the demands made on them.

But the crowds preceded Him, and instead of finding solitude, quiet, and rest, He found great multitudes eager to see, to hear, and to be healed. His compassionate heart was moved. The ripened harvests needed laborers.

He did not call these laborers all at once, but He encouraged the disciples to take themselves to God in prayer, asking Him to send forth laborers into His harvest.

Dear Father, grant me a compassionate heart like Jesus. Help me to see ripened hearts that are ready to receive Your Son into their lives. Amen.

October 4

Prayer That Waits

Let them give thanks to the LORD for His unfailing love and His wonderful deeds for men, for He satisfies the thirsty and fills the hungry with good things.
Psalm 107:8-9

There are many great misconceptions of the true elements and functions of prayer. There are many who earnestly desire to obtain an answer to their prayers, but who go unrewarded and unblessed.

They fix their minds on some great promise of God. This fixing of the mind on something great may help in strengthening faith. But persistent and urgent prayer – prayer that waits until faith increases – must be added to this promise.

Who is able and competent to do such praying except the person who readily, cheerfully and continually *obeys* God?

Thank You, Lord, that You satisfy and fill us with good things. I fix my eyes on You as I pray for a more obedient heart. Amen.

The Fruit of Prayer Is ... Faith!

*You will keep in perfect peace him whose
mind is steadfast, because he trusts in You.*
Isaiah 26:3

Faith is the attitude as well as the act of a soul surrendered to God. His Word and His Spirit dwell in that soul.

It is true that faith must exist in some form or another in order to bring forth praying. But in its strongest form and in its greatest results, faith is the fruit of prayer.

It is true that faith increases the ability and efficiency of prayer. It is likewise true that prayer increases the ability and efficiency of faith.

Prayer and faith work, act, and react together.

Loving Father, I surrender my soul to You. Guide me in Your truth and lead me in the way everlasting. Amen.

Moving Compassion

*When He saw the crowds, He had
compassion on them, because they were harassed
and helpless, like sheep without a Shepherd.*
Matthew 9:36

First, He saw the crowds with their hunger and helpless condition; then He felt compassion that moved Him to pray for the crowds.

Hard is the person, and far from being Christ-like, who sees the multitudes but is unmoved at the sight of their sad state, their unhappiness, and their distress. He has no heart of prayer for others.

Compassion may not always move people, but it should always move toward others. And where it is most helpless to relieve the needs of others, it can at least pray earnestly to God for other people.

Father God, I don't want to be unmoved at the sight of crowds desperately needing Your healing touch. Where I can relieve the needs of others, please help me and where I can't, help me pray. Amen.

October 7

Superhuman

I can do everything through Him who gives me strength.
Philippians 4:13

Obedience to God helps faith as no other attribute possibly can. When a person recognizes the validity and supremacy of God's divine commands, faith in God becomes an easy task. Obedience to God makes it easy to believe and trust God.

Where the spirit of obedience totally saturates the soul, and the will is perfectly surrendered to God, faith becomes a reality. Faith then becomes almost involuntary. After obedience it is the next natural step.

The difficulty in prayer then is not faith, but obedience, which is faith's foundation.

I want my faith in You, Lord, to be a living reality. Make me an obedient servant of You so that Your name may be glorified over all the earth. Amen.

October 8

Trust and Obey

Those who know Your name will trust in You, for You,
Lord, have never forsaken those who seek You.
Psalm 9:10

If we want to pray well and get the most out of our praying, we must look at our obedience. This brings us closer to God.

Disobedient living produces extremely poor praying. No man can pray – really pray – who does not obey.

Our will must be surrendered to God as a primary condition to all successful praying. Everything about us receives its coloring from our innermost character.

Our will determines our character and controls our conduct. We've "simply got to trust and obey. *There's no other way* to be happy in Jesus – but to trust and *obey!"*

*H*eavenly Father, I surrender my will to You. You will give joy and happiness if we only obey and trust in You. Amen.

Spiritual Compassion

Even in darkness light dawns for the upright, for the gracious and compassionate and righteous man.
Psalm 112:4

We are speaking particularly about spiritual compassion here, that which is born in a renewed heart.

This compassion has in it the quality of mercy, is sympathetic, and moves the soul with a feeling of tenderness for others.

Compassion is moved at the sight of sin, sorrow, and suffering. It stands at the other extreme to indifference to the wants and woes of others. It is far removed from insensibility and hardness of heart in the midst of need and trouble.

Compassion stands beside sympathy for others, is interested in them, and is concerned about them.

Almighty God, there where I see suffering, sin and sorrow in the world, make me Your hands and feet to help those thirsty for You. Amen.

October 10

Doing the Will of the Father

Holy, blameless, pure, set apart from sinners.
Hebrews 7:26

Our Lord Jesus Christ, had ready access to God in prayer. He had this free, full access because of His unquestioning obedience to His Father.

Throughout His earthly life His supreme desire was to do the will of His Father. This fact, as well as others – the consciousness of having His life ordered this way – gave Him confidence and assurance.

It enabled Him to draw near to the throne of grace with unlimited confidence born of obedience, promised acceptance, audience and answer.

Loving obedience puts us where we can ask anything in His name. It gives us the assurance that He will do it.

I draw near to Your throne in loving obedience and in awe at Your goodness, Father God. Thank You for the assurance that if we draw near to You, You will draw near to us. Amen.

Compassion of the Soul

"Go, I wish you well, keep warm and well fed."
James 2:16

There is a certain compassion that is inborn to man, that gives simple gifts to those in need.

But spiritual compassion, the kind born in a renewed heart that is Christlike in nature, is deeper, broader, and more prayerlike. The compassion of Christ always moves to prayer.

Compassion is not blind. He who has compassion of the soul has eyes, first of all to see the things that excite compassion. He who has no eyes to see the exceeding sinfulness of sin, the wants and the sorrows of humanity, will never have compassion for humanity.

Dear Father, please open my eyes to the sinfulness and the hurt in this world. I want to make a difference in the lives of people so that Your name may be glorified. Guide me please. Amen.

October 12

Praying and Doing

*"Not everyone who says to Me, 'Lord, Lord,'
will enter the kingdom of heaven, but only he
who does the will of My Father who is in heaven."*
Matthew 7:21

Remember that true praying is not mere eloquent speech. It does not consist of saying in sweet tones, "Lord, Lord." *Prayer is obedience.* Only those who obey have the right to pray. Behind the praying must be the doing. It is the constant doing of God's will in daily life that gives prayer its potency.

No name, however precious and powerful, can protect and give efficiency to prayer that is unaccompanied by doing God's will. Neither can the doing, without the praying, protect from divine disapproval.

If prayer does not inspire, sanctify, and direct our work, then self-will enters and ruins both the work and the worker.

Almighty God, I pray that through the help of Your indwelling Spirit, my prayers will not merely be sweet tones, but effective words. Amen.

Compassion for Sinners

Because of the LORD's great love we are not consumed, for His compassions never fail.
Lamentations 3:22

Compassion has not only to do with the body and its needs. The soul's distressing state, its needs, and its dangers, all ask for compassion.

The highest state of grace is known by compassion for sinners. This sort of compassion belongs to grace and sees not only the bodies of people, but their immortal spirits – soiled by sin, unhappy without God, and in peril of being lost forever.

When compassion sees dying people hurrying to God, then it breaks out into intercessions for these sinful people.

I praise You, Father God, for Your mercy and compassion. Thank You for the knowledge that Your compassion, mercy and love never fail! Amen.

No Harvests without Prayer

*"Ask the Lord of the harvest, therefore,
to send out workers into His harvest field."*
Matthew 9:38

The church is urged to pray for laborers to be sent into the harvest of the Lord. The scarcity of laborers in the harvest field is due to the fact that the church fails to pray for laborers as Jesus commanded.

God's chosen laborers are the only ones who will truly go, filled with Christlike compassion and Christlike power.

Christ's people on their knees, with Christ's compassion in their hearts for dying people and for needy souls, is the pledge of laborers in numbers and character to meet the needs of earth and the purposes of heaven.

Here I am Lord, Your servant, on my knees before You. Use me to touch the souls of people in need of You. Amen.

God Is Sovereign

"For My thoughts are not your thoughts, neither
are your ways My ways," declares the LORD.
Isaiah 55:8

God is the Sovereign of earth, of heaven, and of the choice of laborers in His harvest. He delegates to no one else.

Prayer honors God as sovereign and moves Him to His wise and holy selection. Prayer gets God to send forth the best candidates and the most fit people and the people best qualified to work in the harvest.

Compassion for the world of sinners redeemed by Christ, will move the church to pray for them and stir the church to pray to the Lord of the harvest to send forth laborers into the harvest field.

Father God, I know that You don't always use the most qualified person to do Your work. Sometimes You use ordinary people like me, and equip them to work in Your harvest. Amen.

October 16

The Great High Priest

For we do not have a high priest who is
unable to sympathize with our weaknesses,
but we have one who has been tempted in every way,
just as we are – yet was without sin.
Hebrews 4:15

What great comfort can fill our hearts when we think of One in heaven who lives to intercede for us. The Lord is compassionate and gracious. He is our Great High Priest.

Moreover, if He is filled with such compassion that it moves Him at the Father's right hand to intercede for us, then in everything we should have the same compassion on others and pray for them regularly.

Just as far as we are compassionate will we be able to pray for others.

Lord Jesus, I want to thank You for interceding for us with the Father. Grant me some of Your compassion for the people around me who are in need. Amen.

A Sacred Place

*May God Himself, the God of peace, sanctify you through
and through. May your whole spirit, soul and body
be kept blameless at the coming of our Lord Jesus Christ.*
1 Thessalonians 5:23

Prayer affects places, times, occasions, and circumstances. It has to do with God and with everything that is related to God.

Prayer has an intimate and special relationship to God's house. A church should be a sacred place, set apart from all unholy and secular uses, for the worship of God. As worship is prayer, the house of God is a place set apart for worship.

It is no common place. It is where God dwells, where He meets with His people, and where He delights in the worship of His saints.

Almighty God, thank You that we can meet with fellow believers at church to worship You and be in Your presence. Help us to keep Your house a sacred place of worship and praise. Amen.

October 18

Perfectly at Home

"It is written," He said to them,
"My house will be called a house of prayer."
Matthew 21:13

Prayer is always welcome in the house of God. When prayer is a stranger there, it stops to be God's house.

Our Lord put particular emphasis on what the church should be when He cast out the buyers and sellers in the temple. He makes prayer the most important thing above all else in the house of God. Those who sidetrack prayer misrepresent the church of God and make it into something less than it is meant to be.

Prayer is perfectly at home in the house of God. It is no stranger or guest; it belongs there. It has a divine appointment to be there.

Father God, hear our prayers as they go up to You when we meet together in church to glorify You. Amen.

The Missionary Spirit

May people ever pray for Him.
Psalm 72:15

Psalm 72 deals prophetically with the Messiah. Prayer would be made for His coming to save man, and prayer would be made for the success of the plan of salvation that Jesus would come to set in motion.

The Spirit of Jesus Christ is the spirit of missions. Our Lord Jesus Christ Himself was the first missionary. His promise and arrival put the first missionary movement in action. The missionary spirit is not simply a phase of the gospel, not just a feature of the plan of salvation, but is its very spirit and life.

Whoever is touched by the Spirit of God is inspired to spread the Good News all over the world.

Touch me with Your Spirit, God, so that others may see more of Jesus in me. Amen.

October 20

Fears of Tomorrow

"Therefore do not worry about tomorrow."
Matthew 6:34

The word *worry* implies being drawn in different directions, distracted, anxious, disturbed, upset in spirit. Jesus had warned against this very thing in the Sermon on the Mount.

He was trying to show His people the true secret of a quiet mind, freed from anxiety and unnecessary worry about food and clothing. Tomorrow's evils were not to be considered.

In warning against the fears of tomorrow, evils and the material wants of the body, our Lord was teaching the great lesson of complete and childlike confidence in God.

Dear Lord, thank You for the great lessons we can learn by reading Your Word. Thank You for knowing our every need, and satisfying them all. Amen.

The Holy Place

These things I remember as I pour out my soul:
how I used to go with the multitude, leading
the procession to the house of God, with shouts
of joy and thanksgiving among the festive throng.
Psalm 42:4

Prayer converts the bricks, cement and wood into a sanctuary, a Holy of Holies, where the Lord dwells. Prayer separates the church, in spirit and in purpose, from all other buildings.

With prayer, the house of God becomes a divine sanctuary. So the tabernacle, moving about from place to place, became the Most Holy Place, because God and prayer were there.

Without prayer, the building may be costly, perfect in its structure, attractive to the eye, but it becomes human, with nothing divine in it.

Through our prayers to You, God, we change a building into a sanctuary of worship. Thank You for the great gift of prayer. Amen.

October 22

God-Called Men

Jesus looked at them and said, "With man this is impossible, but not with God; all things are possible with God."
Mark 10:27

If God's people would pray as they ought to pray, the great things that happened in the past would happen again and again. The gospel would advance with a facility and power it has never known.

If Christians prayed as Christians ought, with strong, commanding faith, with earnestness and sincerity, God-called people, God-empowered people, would be burning to go and spread the gospel worldwide. The God-inspired person would go and kindle the flame of sacred fire for Christ, everywhere in all nations.

Soon all people would hear the glad tidings of salvation and have an opportunity to receive Jesus Christ as their personal Savior.

Dear Father, I want to pray as a Christian ought to pray. Please guide me closer to You so that I may hear Your voice and confess Your name wherever I go. Amen.

October 23

A Divine Schoolhouse

*They read from the Book of the Law of God,
making it clear and giving the meaning so that
the people could understand what was being read.*
Nehemiah 8:8

As God's house is a house of prayer, prayer should inspire everything that is done there.

Prayer belongs to every sort of work relating to the church. As God's house is a house of prayer, so it is also a place where shaping praying people out of prayerless people is done.

The house of God is a divine schoolhouse, in which the lesson of prayer is taught, where men and women learn to pray, and where they graduate from the school of prayer.

In Your House, God, do we learn the art of praying. Thank You for revealing more of You through Your Word. Amen.

Anti-Missionary Christians

"You will receive power when the Holy Spirit comes on you; and you will be My witnesses in Jerusalem, and in all Judea and Samaria, and to the ends of the earth."
Acts 1:8

An anti-missionary Christian is a contradiction, as it is impossible to be so. It is impossible for the divine and human forces to put people in such a position not to align them with the missionary cause.

Missionary impulse is the heartbeat of our Lord Jesus Christ sending His own vital forces through the whole body of the church. The spiritual life of God's people rises or falls with the force of those heartbeats.

When these life forces die down, then death follows. Likewise, anti-missionary churches are dead churches, just as anti-missionary Christians are dead Christians.

Lord, I don't want to be an anti-missionary Christian. Ignite the fires of enthusiasm, passion and fervor in my heart so that I will bring You glory. Amen.

A Missionary Age

For Christ's love compels us, because we are convinced
that one died for all, and therefore all died.
2 Corinthians 5:14

We are living in a missionary age. The missionary movement has grown to awaken hope and ignite enthusiasm in the coldest and most lifeless people.

The danger, however, is that the missionary movement will move ahead of the missionary spirit.

This has always been the danger of the church – losing the substance in the shade, losing the spirit, and being satisfied with proclaiming the movement, but not putting the spirit in the movement.

I pray today, God, for all the missionaries out there spreading the gospel. Guide them, protect them and bless them with Your abundant blessings. Amen.

October 26

Private Prayer in Public Worship

*Let everything that has breath
praise the LORD. Praise the LORD.*
Psalm 150:6

The house of God is a holy place for united worship. A quiet room is for individual prayer. Yet even in the house of God, there is the element of private worship.

God's people are to worship Him and pray to Him personally, even in public worship. The church is for the united prayer of God's family, but also for individual believers.

The life, power and glory of the church is prayer. The life of its members is dependent on prayer. The presence of God is secured and retained by prayer. The very place is made sacred by its ministry. Without it, the church is lifeless and powerless.

Loving Father, I want to pray to You on all occasions with all kinds of prayers and requests by the help of Your Spirit. Amen.

Money or Prayer?

And my God will meet all your needs
according to His glorious riches in Christ Jesus.
Philippians 4:19

Many of us have heard earnest speeches stressing the need of money for missions while we have heard perhaps a few stressing the need of prayer.

The common idea among church leaders is that if we get the money, prayer will come. The very opposite is actually true. If we get the church involved in praying, and thus secure the spirit of missions, money will more than likely come as a matter of course.

Spiritual duties and spiritual factors left to the "matter of course" law, will surely die down. Only the things that are stressed live and rule in the spiritual realm.

Thank You for the knowledge and certainty, Father God, that You will meet all our needs abundantly. We only need to ask and pray. Amen.

October 28

Born in the Divine Mind

"I am going to send you what My Father has promised; but stay in the city until you have been clothed with power from on high."
Luke 24:49

Missions mean the bringing of the Gospel to those who have never heard of Christ. It means giving to others the opportunity to hear of salvation through our Lord Jesus Christ, and allowing others to have a chance to receive and accept the blessings of the Gospel.

It means that those who enjoy the benefits of the Gospel give these same religious advantages and gospel privileges to all of mankind. Prayer has a great deal to do with missions.

Both prayer and missions were born in the Divine Mind. Prayer creates and makes missions successful, while the success of missions lean heavily on prayer.

I want to spread the Good News of the Gospel so that others can also have the chance to receive the benefits and blessings that come from Your gracious hand. Amen.

October 29

Praying Creates a Giving Spirit

*Yet for us there is but one God, the Father, from
whom all things came and for whom we live;
and there is but one Lord, Jesus Christ, through
whom all things came and through whom we live.*
1 Corinthians 8:6

The people who give will not necessarily pray. One
of the evils of the present-day missionary movement lies just there. Giving is removed from prayer.
Prayer receives little attention, while giving stands
out. Those who truly pray will be moved to give.

Praying creates a giving spirit. The praying ones
will give liberally and self-denyingly. He who prays
to God will also open his purse to God. But mecha-
nical, reluctant giving kills the very spirit of prayer.

Emphasizing the material and neglecting the
spiritual disregards the spiritual.

*Almighty God, I pray that You will open my eyes
and my heart to people in need of material and spiritual
things. Guide me through Your Holy Spirit. Amen.*

The Grace of Giving

For Zion's sake I will not keep silent, for Jerusalem's sake I will not remain quiet, till her righteousness shines out like the dawn, her salvation like a blazing torch.
Isaiah 62:1

It is truly astonishing how great a part money plays in the modern religious movements and how little part prayer plays.

In striking contrast with that statement, it is marvelous what small part money played in early Christianity as a factor in spreading the Gospel, and how wonderful a part prayer played in it. The grace of giving is nowhere refined more than spending quiet time with God in prayer.

The spreading of Christ's Kingdom lies in regular prayer, and not in the offering box.

I realize again today, heavenly Father, that prayer can change things. Our prayers move You, Lord. Let money not become too important in my life; I want You in first place. Amen.

October 31

November

Pray in Seasons of Conflict

Pray in the Spirit on all occasions
with all kinds of prayers and requests.
Ephesians 6:18

The description of the Christian soldier given by Paul in Ephesians 6 is compact and comprehensive. He is seen as always being in the seasons of conflict.

There are seasons of prosperity and adversity, victory and defeat. He is to pray in all seasons and with all prayer. This is to be added to the armor when he goes into battle. The Christian soldier, if he fights to win, must pray fervently.

Only in this way is he able to defeat his long-standing enemy, the Devil, and his many agents. To pray on all occasions is the divine direction given to all Christ's soldiers.

*D*ear God, I know that I am more than a conqueror through Christ's love for us. I must only pray if I want to win the battle. Help me please. Amen.

November 1

Idle Church Members

In the name of the Lord Jesus Christ, we command you,
brothers, to keep away from every brother who does not
live according to the teaching you received from us.
2 Thessalonians 3:6

As good as the church at Thessalonica was, it also needed instruction and caution on this matter of looking after those who did not live according to the teachings.

It is not the mere presence of idle persons in a church that causes God's displeasure. It is when they are tolerated and no steps are taken to either cure them of their evil practices, or exclude them from the fellowship of the church.

This carelessness regarding the wayward members on the part of the church is but a sad sign of a lack of praying.

Father, guide us, Your church, not to neglect those who are not living according to Your teachings. Let us be a helping hand to them in turning back to You. Amen.

November 2

The Christian Life Is Warfare

Endure hardship with us
like a good soldier of Christ Jesus.
2 Timothy 2:3

What a misconception many people have of the Christian life! The average church member today does not seem to know anything about conflict or how the world, the Devil and flesh will try to hinder a believer's walk.

It is just at this point in today's Christianity that one may find its greatest defect. There is little or nothing of the soldier element in it. The discipline, self-denial, spirit of hardship and determination so prominent in and belonging to the military life, are lacking.

Yet the Christian life is warfare. We need to fight the good fight and endure hardships as good soldiers of Christ.

Almighty Father, please strengthen me to endure hardships of many kinds like a good soldier of Christ. Amen.

November 3

Disorderly Conduct

*Brothers, if someone is caught in a sin, you who
are spiritual should restore him gently.
But watch yourself, or you also may be tempted.*
Galatians 6:1

The church is an organization for mutual help, and
it is charged with the watchful care of all of its members. Unruly behavior cannot pass by unnoticed.

The work of the church is not just to seek members, but to watch over and guard them after they
have entered the church. If someone starts following the path of sin, members of the church should
try to redirect that person to God's way.

However, if someone knowingly chooses to
sin, then that person should be removed from the
church. This is the doctrine our Lord lays down for
us, His church.

*I pray, heavenly Father, that people shall see Your
church as a safe haven and a place of rest and comfort.
Guide Your church in their work to guard and watch
over Your people. Amen.*

November 4

Supplication

Pray in the Spirit on all occasions with all kinds
of prayers and requests. With this in mind,
be alert and always keep on praying for all the saints.
Ephesians 6:18

The power of prayer is most forceful on the battle-field in the midst of the noise and strife of conflict. Paul was pre-eminently a soldier of the cross. His strength was almost gone. What reinforcements could he count on?

It was a critical moment in the conflict. What strength could be added to the energy of his own prayers? The answer lies in the prayers of others; his fellow believers.

These, he believed, will bring him additional aid. He could then win his fight, overcome his adversaries, and, ultimately, prevail.

Loving Father, in the midst of the hustle-and-bustle, I become still before You. Refresh my soul, strengthen my faith and help me fight the good fight for Your glory. Amen.

Selfish Praying

*When you ask, you do not receive, because
you ask with wrong motives, that you may
spend what you get on your pleasures.*
James 4:3

The soldier's prayer must reflect his profound concern for the success and well-being of the whole army. The battle is not altogether a personal matter.

Victory cannot be achieved for self alone. The cause of God, His saints, their woes and trials, their duties and crosses, all should find a pleading voice in the Christian soldier when he prays.

He dare not limit his praying to himself. Selfish praying is the quickest way to dry up spiritual blessings. Pray with God's whole army and His perfect will in mind.

Father God, when I pray I want my motives to be pure and right. Please guide me when I pray not to pray selfish prayers, but to have Your perfect will in mind. Amen.

Watchfulness

"Watch and pray."
Matthew 26:41

The Christian soldier is compelled to constant guard duty. He is faced with an enemy who never sleeps, who is always alert, and who is ever prepared to take advantage of the fortunes of war.

Watchfulness is a fundamental principle of Christ's warriors. They cannot dare to be asleep at their posts. Such a lapse brings them not only under the displeasure of the Captain of their salvation, but also exposes them to added danger.

Watchfulness, therefore, is a necessity for a soldier of the Lord.

Lord, You tell us in Your Word to watch and pray so that we may not fall into temptation. Make me a worthy soldier of Your army. Amen.

Watch, Watch, Watch!

Pray in the Spirit on all occasions
with all kinds of prayers and requests.
Ephesians 6:18

In the New Testament, there are three different meanings for the word "watch." The first means "absence of sleep" and implies a wakeful frame of mind. The second meaning is to be "fully awake" – through carelessness or laziness, something horrible could suddenly happen. The third means "to be calm and collected in spirit," cautious against all pitfalls and distractions.

All three definitions are used by Paul. Two of them are used in connection with prayer. Watchfulness must guard and cover the whole spiritual man and prepare him for prayer. Everything resembling unpreparedness or non-vigilance is death to prayer.

Father, I realize that it is important to watch and pray always because our enemy prowls around like a hungry lion. Help me, Lord, to resist the Devil. Amen.

November 8

Alert Soldiers

On reaching the place, He said to them,
"Pray that you will not fall into temptation."
Luke 22:40

The Christian soldier must be as intense in his praying as in his fighting, for his victories will depend much more on his praying than on his fighting.

Prayer and supplication must strengthen the armor of God. The Holy Spirit must aid the supplication with His own zealous plea. And the soldier must pray in the Spirit.

In this, as in all other forms of warfare, eternal vigilance is the price of victory. Thus, watchfulness and perseverance must mark every activity of the Christian warrior.

God, make me a Christian warrior who depends greatly on my prayers to You. Make me watchful and perseverant through the help of Your Spirit. Amen.

Intercession

*"For where two or three come together
in My name, there am I with them."*
Matthew 18:20

The pious Quesnel said that "God is found in union
and agreement. Nothing is more efficacious than
this in prayer."

Intercession combines with prayers and suppli-
cations. The word *intercession* does not necessarily
mean "prayer in relation to others." It means "a
coming together, a falling in with a most intimate
friend for free, unrestrained communion."

It implies free prayer, familiar and bold. This passage represents the church in prayer. The strength
of the church is in prayer.

*Thank You, Lord, for the knowledge we have that
where two or three come together in Your name, You will
be there with them. I praise Your holy name. Amen.*

Church Discipline

*"If he refuses to listen to them, tell it to the church,
treat him as you would a pagan or a tax collector."*
Matthew 18:17

Discipline in church, now a lost art in the modern church, must go hand in hand with prayer. The church that has no disposition to separate wrong-doers from the church, will have no communication with God.

Church purity must precede the church's prayers. The unity of discipline in the church precedes the unity of prayers by the church. Take note of the fact that a church that is careless in discipline will be careless in praying.

The need of watchfulness over the lives of its members belongs to the church of God.

Dear Father, I pray for Your churches around the world to not be careless in their disciplines so that their prayers will not become careless. Amen.

Fighting Qualities

Therefore put on the full armor of God,
so that when the day of evil comes,
you may be able to stand your ground.
Ephesians 6:13

The Christian soldier who is bent on defeating the Devil must possess a clear idea of the character of the life into which he has entered.

He must know something of his enemies – their strengths, their skills, their viciousness. Knowing something of the character of the enemy and realizing the need of preparation to overcome them, will be of great help to withstand the enemy when the day of evil comes.

How can the brave warrior for Christ be made braver still? Prayer, and more prayer, adds to the fighting qualities and the more certain victories of God's good, fighting people.

I know that it is only through diligent prayer to You, God, that I can become a good, fighting soldier for You. Help me to never stop praying. Amen.

Godly Decline

*"I know your deeds, your hard work and your perseverance.
I know that you cannot tolerate wicked men."*
Revelation 2:2

It is somewhat striking that the church at Ephesus, though it had left its first love and had sadly declined in vital godliness and in the things that make up spiritual life, still received credit for this good quality of not tolerating wicked men.

At the same time, the church at Pergamos was given a warning because the beliefs of some members were stumbling blocks for other members.

The impression is that the church leaders were blind to the presence of such hurtful characters. There was no concerted prayer effort to cleanse the church and keep it clean. A praying church should be quick to help a fallen member.

Dear God, I pray for Your churches all over the world to be praying churches who are keen to help fellow believers and lead and guide them. Amen.

Fighting the Good Fight

Fight the good fight of the faith. Take hold of the eternal
life to which you were called when you made your
good confession in the presence of many witnesses.
1 Timothy 6:12

Christian soldiers, fighting the good fight of faith, have access to a place of retreat where they continually go to for prayer.

It cannot be said too often that the life of a Christian is warfare, an intense conflict, a lifelong contest. The Bible calls people to life, not a picnic or holiday. It requires effort, wrestling, and struggling. It demands full energy of the spirit to withstand the enemy and to come out, in the end, more than a conqueror.

It is not an easy rose-lined path. From start to finish, it is war.

Thank You, loving Father, that we can come to You
to find rest and strength for our souls in the constant
battle we are fighting against the enemy. We are more
than conquerors through Your great love for us. Amen.

November 14

Without Prayer, We Are Easy Prey!

Be self-controlled and alert. Your enemy the devil prowls around like a roaring lion looking for someone to devour.
1 Peter 5:8

God's church is a militant host. It fights against unseen forces of evil. God's people form an army fighting to establish His Kingdom on the earth. Their aim is to destroy the sovereignty of Satan and, over its ruins, erect the kingdom of God.

The entire life of a Christian soldier is dependent on a life of prayer.

Without prayer – no matter what else he has – the Christian soldier's life will be feeble and ineffective. Without prayer, he is an easy prey for his spiritual enemies.

Father God, I don't want to be an easy target for the enemy. Help me to be self-controlled and alert, and to always come to You, for You renew my strength. Amen.

Quantity or Quality Membership?

"Who is blind but my servant?"
Isaiah 42:19

There is a blindness in the church with regard to members choosing a life of sin over God's way of life.

The truth is, there is such a lust for members in the church, that the officials have entirely lost sight of the members who are living in open disregard of God's Word. The idea now is quantity in membership, not quality.

Prayer can change this. Through prayer, members would either confess their sins, or leave the church.

I pray, God, that You will open the eyes of Your people. Especially those in leadership positions in Your church so that they will focus more on quality than quantity of members. Amen.

November 16

Church Export Products

"Your kingdom come, Your will
be done on earth as it is in heaven."
Matthew 6:10

The missionary movement in the apostolic church was born in an atmosphere of fasting and prayer. Missionary work is God's work.

Praying missionaries are needed for the work, and only a praying church can send them out. Prayer has the ability to make the spreading of the gospel so much more powerful.

The energy to give the gospel momentum and conquering power over all its enemies is the energy of prayer.

Spreading Your gospel across the world depends on the prayers of Your children. Make us strong, Lord, and grant us the energy to make things happen through our prayers to You. Amen.

The Divine Plan

To the weak I became weak, to win the weak.
I have become all things to all men
so that by all possible means I might save some.
1 Corinthians 9:22

Our Lord's plan for securing workers in the missionary field is the same as His plan for obtaining preachers. It is through the process of praying.

It is the prayer plan as distinguished from all man-made plans. These mission workers are to be "sent people". God must send them. They are God-called, divinely moved to this great work. They are inwardly moved to enter the harvest fields of the world.

People do not choose to be missionaries any more than they choose to be preachers. God sends out laborers in His harvest fields in answer to the prayers of His church.

Thank You, Almighty God, that You call missionaries to the harvest field in answer to the prayers of Your church. Amen.

November 18

Praying Missionaries

*He saw that there was no one, he was
apalled that there was no one to intervene.*
Isaiah 59:16

A praying church brings about laborers in the harvest field of the world. It is the church's responsibility to pray for missionaries.

It is all right to send trained people to the foreign field, but first of all they must be God-sent. The sending is the fruit of prayer. As praying people pray for workers to be sent, so in turn the workers themselves must be praying people. The prime mission of these praying missionaries is to convert prayerless, heathen people into praying people.

Prayer can help people fulfill their calling, their divine credentials, and their work.

God, my prayer today is for all the missionaries out in the field spreading Your Word. Bless them and keep them and grant them Your peace. Amen.

Fitness in Prayer

For physical training is of some value,
but godliness has value for all things, holding
promise for both the present life and the life to come.
1 Timothy 4:8

If you are not a praying man here at home you need to develop fitness in prayer in order to become a missions worker abroad.

If you are not compassionate towards people around you, how can you have compassion for people abroad? Missionaries are not believers who are failures at home. A person must first be a person of prayer at home before becoming a missionary and pray overseas.

In other words, it takes the same spiritual qualifications for being a home missions worker as it does for being a foreign missions worker.

Wherever I am, Father God, be it at my home or somewhere abroad, I need to be a missionary for You. Guide me in this task through Your Spirit. Amen.

God's Called People

*"Ask the Lord of the harvest, therefore,
to send out workers into His harvest field."*
Matthew 9:38

God in His own way, in answer to the prayers, calls believers to His harvest fields. People should be called to be missionaries. They must not just feel obliged to go because of pressure from their church or missionary board. They must be chosen by God.

Is the harvest great? Are the laborers few? Pray! Oh, that a great wave of prayer would sweep over the church, asking God to send out laborers into the needy harvest fields!

There is no danger of the Lord sending out too many laborers and crowding the fields. If He calls you, He will equip you.

Dear God, help us not to send people to the harvest field independent of Your call. We only need to pray, You will prepare Your workers. Amen.

November 21

Faith That God Is Able

"When the Son of man comes,
will He find faith on the earth?"
Luke 18:8

The possibilities of prayer are measured by faith in God's ability to do. Faith is the one prime condition by which God works and is the one prime condition by which man prays.

Faith believes in God's limitless power. Faith gives character to prayer. A feeble faith has always brought forth feeble praying. Vigorous faith creates vigorous praying. We need a quickening faith in God's power.

We have restricted God to fit into our world, and now we have little faith in His power. We have made Him a little God through our little faith.

I pray, God, that You will increase my faith in Your ability to accomplish anything. What is impossible for man is possible with You. Glory to Your name. Amen.

God's Ability to Do!

"If You can do anything, take pity on us and help us."
Mark 9:22

The only condition that restricts God's power making Him unable to act is a lack of faith. He is not limited in action nor restrained by the conditions that limit people. God is never limited.

The conditions of time, place, nearness, ability and all others that could possibly be named, have no bearing on God. If God's children will look to Him and cry to Him with true prayer, He will hear and will deliver, no matter how dire their circumstances.

It is strange how God has to school His people in His ability to do all things!

Father God, we are not restricted by time, place or ability to do great things for You. The only thing restricting us is our lack of prayer. Make me a praying warrior. Amen.

Above Human Thought

Now to Him who is able to do
immeasurebly more than all we ask or imagine.
Ephesians 3:20

Prayer has to do with God, with His ability to do.

In God's ability to do, He goes far beyond man's ability to ask. Human thoughts, human words, human imaginations, human desires, and human needs cannot in any way measure God's ability to do.

Prayer goes forward by the power of God Himself. Prayer goes forth with faith, not only in the promise of God, but also in God Himself and in His ability to do.

I thank You, Lord, for the knowledge in Your Word that You are able to do immeasurably more than we can ask or imagine. To You be all the glory forever and ever. Amen.

November 24

The Majesty of God

"Forget the former things, do not dwell on the past."
Isaiah 43:18

Every day we see the majesty and power of God in His Creation. This should be the basis of our faith in God and should help us in our prayers.

Then God calls us away from what He has done and turns our minds to Himself personally. The infinite glory and power of His person are set before us to meditate on.

Therefore, if we have prayer and faith, He will so answer our prayers and so work in us that His former work shall not be remembered. What lies ahead for us in God's plan will be much greater.

Almighty God, my prayer to You today is for increased faith and perseverance in prayer. I want to bring glory to You through my life. Amen.

November 25

The House of God

Let us not give up meeting together,
as some are in the habit of doing.
Hebrews 10:25

Without prayer, a church is like a body without spirit; it is a dead, lifeless thing. A church with prayer in it has God in it. When prayer is set aside, God is also set aside. When prayer becomes an unfamiliar exercise, then God Himself is a stranger there.

As God's house is a house of prayer, the divine intention is that people should leave their homes and go to meet Him in His house.

God has promised to meet His people there. It is their duty to go there for that specific reason. Prayer should be the chief attraction for all spiritually-minded churchgoers.

I pray, Lord God, that Your church would never stop meeting together. But will come together to worship You. Amen.

November 26

God Gives Freely

*He who did not spare His own Son, but gave
Him up for us all – how will He not also, along
with Him, graciously give us all things?*
Romans 8:32

What a basis we have here for prayer and faith! The promise to give us *"all things"* is backed by the fact that God gave His one and only Son for our redemption.

We can therefore come to God with our requests and ask boldly and confidently.

The more faith we have in God to supply our needs, the more grace He will give us and we will see His glory. When you pray, believe that God is able to freely give you all things.

Father God, I believe that You are able to freely give me all good things. Thank You for Your mercy and grace. Amen.

Christ's Intercession

Pray continually.
1 Thessalonians 5:17

How enthroned, magnificent, and royal is the intercession of our Lord Jesus Christ at His Father's right hand in heaven!

The benefits of His intercession flow to us through our intercessions. Our intercession should connect to a plan greater than our own – God's plan. His business and His life are to pray. Our business and our lives ought to be to pray too and failure in our intercession affects the fruit of His intercession.

Lazy, heartless, feeble, and indifferent praying hinders the effects of Christ's praying on our behalf.

Lord God, just like Jesus, I want the business of my life to be to pray. Please guide me through the power of Your Spirit. Amen.

November 28

The History of Prayer

Trust in the LORD and do good;
dwell in the land and enjoy safe pastures.
Psalm 37:3

The possibilities of prayer are established by the facts and the history of prayer. Facts are stubborn things. Facts are true things.

Theories may be but speculations. Opinions may be wrong. But facts are reliable. They cannot be ignored. What are the possibilities of prayer judged by the facts? What is the history of prayer? What does it reveal to us? Prayer has a history, written in God's Word and recorded in the experiences and lives of God's saints.

History is truth teaching by example. We may miss the truth by perverting the history, but the truth is in the facts of history.

Thank You, Father, that there is proof in Your Word of the possibilities and power of prayer. Thank You that I can know the Truth, and that the Truth sets me free. Amen.

God and History

Commit your way to the LORD;
trust in Him and He will do this. He will make
your righteousness shine like the noonday sun.
Psalm 37:5-6

God reveals Himself through the facts of religious history. God teaches us His will by the facts and examples of Bible history. God has ruled the world by prayer and He still rules the world in the same divinely ordained way.

The possibilities of prayer cover not only individuals but also cities and nations. The praying of Moses was the one thing that stood between the wrath of God against the Israelites, and the execution of that divine purpose.

Nineveh was saved because the king and its people repented of their evil ways and gave themselves to prayer and fasting.

Father, through the facts of religious history in the Bible we can learn much about Your character. You are great and mighty in power. I praise Your name. Amen.

December

December

God's Will Be Done

*Let the Word of Christ dwell in you richly as
you teach and admonish one another with all wisdom,
and as you sing psalms, hymns and spiritual
songs with gratitude in your hearts to God.*
Colossians 3:16

God's Word is a record of prayer – of praying people and their achievements. No one can read the instances, commands, and examples of statements that concern themselves with prayer, without realizing that the cause of God and the success of His work in this world are committed to prayer. People who don't, have never been used by Him.

A reverence for God's holy name is closely related to a high regard for His Word. This hallowing of God's name, the ability to do His will on earth as it is done in heaven, and the establishment and glory of God's Kingdom are as much involved in prayer as when Jesus taught men the Lord's Prayer.

Dear God, I realize that much of the successes in my life depend on my prayers to You and meditating on Your Word. Thank You for the gift of prayer. Amen.

December 1

Midway Between God and Man

*During the days of Jesus' life on earth, He offered
up prayers and petitions with loud cries and tears.*
Hebrews 5:7

True prayer links itself to the will of God and runs
in streams of compassion and intercession for all
people.

As Jesus Christ died for all people so prayer
gives itself for the benefit of all people. Like our
Mediator between God and people, he who prays
stands midway between God and people.

Prayer holds the movements of believers in its
grasp and embraces the destinies of believers for all
eternity. It touches heaven and moves earth. Prayer
connects earth to heaven and brings heaven in close
contact with earth.

*Father, thank You that true praying links us to Your
will. Thank You that it can touch heaven and move
earth. Amen.*

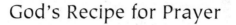

God's Recipe for Prayer

Through faith ... gained what was promised.
Hebrews 11:33

Under certain circumstances, persistent prayer can bring additional assurance of God's promises. There would seem to be the capacity in prayer for going beyond the Word, beyond His promise, and into the very presence of God Himself.

Jacob wrestled, not so much with a promise as with the Promiser. We must take hold of the Promiser, or else the promise is without purpose. Prayer may well be defined as the force that vitalizes and energizes the Word of God, by taking hold of God Himself. By taking hold of the Promiser, prayer releases the personal promise.

God, thank You that You are always faithful to Your promises. Amen.

December 3

Prayer Privileges

Seek the LORD while He may be found; call on Him while He is near. Let the wicked forsake his way and the evil man his thoughts. Let him turn to the LORD, and He will have mercy on him, and to our God, for He will freely pardon.
Isaiah 55:6-7

As there is no difference in the kind of sin people find themselves in, everybody needs the saving grace of God.

Further, as this saving grace is obtained only in answer to prayer, people are therefore called to pray because of their very needs.

It is a privilege for every follower of God to pray, but it is also a duty for him to call upon God. God shows mercy to all sinners. All are welcome to approach the throne of grace with all their wants and needs; with all their sins and burdens.

Father God, thank You for the great privilege of prayer. But I also know that as a Christian it is my duty to pray. Thank You for Your mercy and grace. Amen.

Fuel for Life

*"It is written: 'Man does not live on bread alone, but on
every word that comes from the mouth of God.'"*
Matthew 4:4

The Word of God is put into action by the process
and practice of prayer. If it is written in our hearts, it
will form an outflowing current of prayer.

Promises, stored in the heart, are the fuel from
which prayer receives life and warmth. Just as coal
which has been stored in the earth gives us comfort
on stormy days and cold nights, the Word of God
stored in our hearts is the food by which prayer is
nourished and strengthened.

Prayer, like people, cannot live by bread alone.

*Dear heavenly Father, I know that I cannot live on
bread alone, but rather on every word that comes from
Your mouth. Amen.*

Blessed to Bless

*"I tell you the truth, anyone who has faith in Me will
do what I have been doing. He will do even greater
things than these, because I am going to the Father."*
John 14:12

Prayer joined with loving obedience is the answer
to all ends and all things. Prayer joined to the Word
of God makes all God's gifts sacred.

Prayer is not simply to receive things from God,
but to make those things holy that have already
been received from Him. It is not merely to *receive* a
blessing, but also to be able to *give* a blessing. Prayer
makes common things holy and worldly things sacred.

Prayer receives things from God with thanksgiving and hallows them with thankful hearts and
devoted service.

*I thank You, Almighty God, that prayer and loving obedience are the answer to all things in this life. I
praise You for all the blessings received from Your hand.
Amen.*

God's Word in Our Hearts

*For everything God created is good, and nothing is
to be rejected if it is received with thanksgiving, because
it is consecrated by the word of God and prayer.*
1 Timothy 4:4-5

God's good gifts are holy, not only because of God's creative power, but because they are made holy by prayer.

Doing God's will is essential for effectual praying. You may ask, how are we to know what God's will is? The answer is by studying His Word and by letting the Word dwell in us richly.

It shows us that we cannot only do the will of God externally, but from the heart, without holding back from the intimate presence of the Lord.

By meditating on Your Word and keeping it in our hearts, we can know what Your will is. I want to be in Your presence constantly, so that I can do Your will. Amen.

Filled with God's Spirit

*He is always wrestling in prayer for you,
that you may stand firm in all the
will of God, mature and fully assured.*
Colossians 4:12

To know God's will in prayer, we must be filled with God's Spirit, who intercedes for the saints.

To be filled with God's Spirit and to be filled with God's Word, is to know God's will. It is to be put in such a state of heart that it will enable us to read and correctly interpret the purposes of the eternal.

Filling our hearts with the Word and the Spirit gives us an insight into the will of the Father. It enables us to discern His will and to make it the guide and compass of our lives.

My prayer today God, is to be filled with Your Spirit, so that I may know Your will. You are the guide and compass of my life. Amen.

The Universality of Prayer

May the God of hope fill you with all joy and peace
as you trust in Him, so that you may overflow
with hope by the power of the Holy Spirit.
Romans 15:13

Prayer has far-reaching and worldwide effects. Prayer goes everywhere and lays its hand upon everything. There is a universality in prayer.

Prayer is individual in its application and benefits, but it is general and worldwide at the same time in its good influences. Prayer blesses man in every event of life, provides help in every emergency, and gives comfort in every trouble.

There is no experience that people need to face without prayer as a helper, a comforter, and a guide.

Thank You for the great gift of prayer. We can face every situation in life through our prayers to You. You will answer us and comfort us. Amen.

December 9

Scriptural Authority

Faith comes from hearing the message, and
the message is heard through the Word of Christ.
Romans 10:17

By scriptural authority, prayer may be divided into the petition of faith and that of submission. The prayer of faith is based on the written Word, for it inevitably receives its answer – the very thing for which it prays.

The prayer of submission is without a definite word of promise, so to speak. But it takes hold of God with a remorseful spirit and pleads with Him for that which the soul desires.

Abraham had no definite promise that God would spare Sodom. But the devoted leader gained his plea with God when he interceded for the Israelites with persistent prayers and many tears.

Through persistent prayers and many tears Abraham interceded for the Israelites and gained his plea. Thank You, Father, that You always hear our prayers and will answer them in good time. Amen.

Call on God's Name

For there is no difference ... the same Lord is
Lord of all and richly blesses all who call on Him.
Romans 10:12-13

When we speak of the universality of prayer, we discover many sides to it. First, it is important that all people should pray.

Prayer is intended for all people, because all people need God and need what God has and what only prayer can give. As people are called upon to pray everywhere, they need to pray for others everywhere.

Universal terms are used when believers are commanded to pray. There is a promise in universal terms to all who call upon God for pardon, for mercy and help.

I praise You, loving Father, for the knowledge we have that we can pray to You anywhere and at any time. Amen.

December 11

The Prayer Environment

I want men everywhere to lift up holy hands
in prayer, without anger or disputing.
1 Timothy 2:8

God's children can pray everywhere, since God is accessible in every climate and under all circumstances. There is just one modification of this idea.

Some places exist in which evil business is conducted. The intrinsic environments of these settings grow out of the places, out of the moral character of those who do business there, and out of those who support them. In such places, prayer would not be appropriate.

Prayer is so much out of place at such places that no one would ever presume to pray there.

Thank You, God, for being accessible to us in every climate and under all circumstances. But make us aware of the fact that prayer is more appropriate in some places than others. Amen.

Where to Pray

"Everything is permissible for me" – but not everything is beneficial. "Everything is permissible for me" – but I will not be mastered by anything.
1 Corinthians 6:12

While we are to pray everywhere, it means that we should not visit places where we cannot pray.

To pray everywhere is to pray in all legitimate places, and to attend especially those places where prayer is welcome. To pray everywhere is to preserve the spirit of prayer in places of business, in our dealings with people, and in the privacy of the home.

The model prayer of our Lord is the universal prayer because it is adapted to all people everywhere and in all times of need.

I want to thank You, Lord, for giving us an example in Your Word of how we ought to pray. Amen.

Pray for Those in Authority

I urge, then, first of all, that requests, prayers,
intercessions and thanksgiving be made for everyone –
for kings and all those in authority, that we may live
peaceful and quiet lives in all godliness and holiness.
1 Timothy 2:1-2

It is especially important to pray regularly for our church leaders. Prayer has mighty power.

It makes good rulers, and makes good rulers better rulers. It restrains the lawless and the despotic. Rulers are to be prayed for. They are not out of reach and control of prayer, because they are not out of reach and control of God.

Wicked Nero was on the throne of Rome when Paul wrote these words to Timothy urging prayer for those in authority, so that peace and quiet could reign in the land.

God, I know that prayer is far-reaching in its effects.
I pray today for all the people in leadership positions all
over the world that they will know and follow You as
the divine Leader and King. Amen.

December 14

Vital Force of Prayer

"If you believe, you will receive
whatever you ask for in prayer."
Matthew 21:22

Unless the power of prayer is supplied by God's Word, prayer, though earnest, is empty.

The absence of power in praying can be traced to the absence of a constant supply of God's Word to repair the waste and renew the life. He who wants to learn to pray well must first study God's Word and store it in his memory and thoughts.

When we consult God's Word, we find that no duty is more binding than that of prayer. No promises are more radiant, more abounding, than those that are attached to prayer.

Father God, I know that I can only learn to pray well by studying Your Word and keeping it in my heart. I want to fulfill the great duty I have of being Your praying servant. Amen.

Big-Hearted Prayers

*The LORD upholds all those who fall
and lifts up all who are bowed down.*
Psalm 145:14

Compassion should be present in our hearts when we pray and people should engage their thoughts in approaching the throne of grace.

No man with narrow views of God, of His plan to save people, and of the universal needs of all people can pray effectively. It takes a broad-minded man who understands God and His purposes in the Atonement to pray well.

Prayer comes from a big heart, filled with thoughts about and sympathies for all people.

Dear God, I know that it takes a broad-minded and big-hearted person who knows Your will to pray well. Please guide me in becoming more like Jesus every day. Amen.

Prayer Brings Heaven to Earth

"I have told you these things, so that in Me
you may have peace. In this world you will have trouble.
But take heart! I have overcome the world."
John 16:33

Prayer runs parallel with the will of God. Prayer reaches up to heaven and brings heaven down to earth. Prayer contains a double blessing.

It rewards the person who prays and blesses him who is prayed for. It brings peace to places of conflict. There is an inner and outer calm that comes to him who prays.

Right praying not only makes life beautiful and peaceful, but it also infuses righteousness. Honesty, integrity and strength of character are the natural and essential fruit of prayer.

Thank You, Lord God, that in You we may have peace. I know that trouble will come my way, but I also know that I need not fear because You have already overcome the world. Amen.

December 17

Our Great Intercessor

*Praise be to the God and Father of our Lord Jesus
Christ, the Father of compassion and the God of all
comfort, who comforts us in all our troubles,
so that we can comfort those in any trouble with
the comfort we ourselves have received from God.*
2 Corinthians 1:3-4

Worldwide, selfless praying pleases God and is acceptable in His sight, because it co-operates with His will and runs in gracious streams to God's people.

It is this kind of praying that Christ Jesus did when He was on earth, and the same kind that He is now doing at His Father's right hand in heaven as our mighty Intercessor.

He is the pattern of prayer. He stands between God and man, the one Mediator who gave Himself as a ransom for each and every person.

*Lord, thank You for loving us so much that You gave
Your only Son so that we could live with You eternally
in heaven. Amen.*

The House of Prayer

"If you remain in Me and My words remain in you,
ask whatever you wish, and it will be given you."
John 15:7

As God's house is called *the house of prayer* because prayer is the most important of its tasks, so the Bible also may be called the book of prayer. Prayer is the great theme of its message to mankind.

As the Word of Christ dwells richly in us, we become transformed. The result is that we become praying Christians.

Faith is constructed of the Word and the Spirit, and faith is the body and substance of prayer. His Word becomes the basis of and the inspiration for our praying.

Lord, You say that if we remain in You and Your Word remains in us, we may ask whatever we wish, and it will be given to us. I praise Your holy name for being so good to us. Amen.

The Endless Possibilities of Prayer

Now to Him who is able to do immeasurably more than all we ask or imagine.
Ephesians 3:20

Paul, in his remarkable prayer for the Ephesians, honored the unlimited possibilities of prayer, and he glorified the ability of God to answer prayer.

Prayer is all-inclusive. There is no time or place that prayer does not cover and sanctify. All things on earth and in heaven, everything for time and for eternity, all are embraced in prayer.

Nothing is too great and nothing is too small to be a subject of prayer. Prayer reaches down to the least things of life and includes the greatest things that concern us.

Dear heavenly Father, I thank You that I can pray to You about anything. Nothing is too great and nothing is too small to bring to You in prayer. Amen.

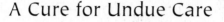

A Cure for Undue Care

*Do not be anxious about anything, but in everything,
by prayer and petition, with thanksgiving present
your requests to God. And the peace of God,
which transcends all understanding, will guard
your hearts and your minds in Christ Jesus.*
Philippians 4:6-7

Worry is the epidemic evil of mankind. Everybody is influenced by worry.

There are the cares of the home, from which there is no escape except in prayer. There are the cares of business, the cares of poverty, and the cares of riches. We live in a fearful world, and we are a fearful race. The caution of Paul is well addressed in Philippians 4:6-7. This is the divine command, so that we might be able to live above anxiety and freed from undue care.

This is the divinely prescribed remedy for all anxiety, all worry, and all troubles.

I know, Lord, that we can bring our cares and burdens to You. You will give us comfort and rest because You care for us. Amen.

December 21

Living Worry-Free

The peace of God, which transcends
all understanding, will guard your hearts.
Philippians 4:7

Only prayer can bring the "peace of God, which transcends all understanding" into the heart and mind (Phil. 4:7).

Cares divide, distract, bewilder, and destroy unity and quietness of mind. What great need to guard against them and learn the one secret of their cure – prayer! Prayer about everything can quiet every distraction, and lift every care from weary lives and from confused hearts.

The specific prayer is the perfect cure for all anxieties, cares, and worries. Only prayer can drive worry away and save from worrying over things that we cannot change.

Father, I bring all my cares, worries and anxieties to You today. I leave them at Your feet. Please give me peace. In Jesus' name I pray. Amen.

The Key of Missionary Success

*"For the Son of Man came to seek
and to save what was lost."*
Luke 19:10

If Satan cannot prevent a great movement for God, his craftiest trick is to try to ruin the movement. Only mighty prayer will save the movement from being materialized and keep the spirit of the movement strong and alive.

The key of all missionary success is prayer. That key is in the hands of the churches. Financial resources are not the real muscles of war in this fight. Machinery carries no power to break down heathen walls and win heathen hearts to Christ.

Prayer alone can accomplish this.

Father God, the key to all missionary success lies in our prayers rising up to You. Guide us and strengthen us to keep on praying even when words fail us. Amen.

December 23

Rejoice Always

Rejoice in the Lord always. I will say it again: Rejoice!
Let your gentleness be evident to all. The Lord is near.
Philippians 4:4-5

In a world filled with all kinds of worry, where temptation is the rule, where there are so many things testing us, how is it possible to rejoice always?

We look at the command to rejoice always, and we accept it and respect it as the Word of God, but no joy comes. We decide to be kind and gentle. We remember the nearness of the Lord, but still we are hasty, quick and impatient.

A joyous, carefree, peaceful experience brings the believer into a joyous living by faith. We should only obey and trust God.

In this broken world we live in, Father, it is difficult to rejoice always. But I know that to live according to Your will, my life will be a joyful experience pleasing in Your sight. Amen.

Prayer That Gets Answers

When you ask, you do not receive, because
you ask with wrong motives, that you
may spend what you get on your pleasures.
James 4:3

Answers to prayer are the only surety we have that we prayed right. What marvelous power there is in prayer! What untold miracles it works in this world! Why is it that the average prayer goes begging for an answer?

God is not playing make-believe in His marvelous promises to answer prayer. The whole explanation is found in our wrong prayers. We ask and do not receive because we ask wrong. Child of God, can you pray? If not, why not? Answered prayer is the proof of your real praying.

Father, when I do not receive an answer to my prayers, let me examine my own motives. Guide me through Your Spirit to pray with an honest and sincere heart. Amen.

December 25

Abiding in Christ

"If you remain in Me and My words remain in you,
ask whatever you wish, and it will be given you."
John 15:7

Are your prayers answered? The efficiency of prayer from a biblical standpoint lies solely in the answer to prayer. The benefit of prayer has been well and popularly maximized by the saying, "It moves the arm that moves the universe."

To get unquestioned answers to prayer is not only important for the satisfying of our desires, but it is also the evidence of our abiding in Christ. Thus, it becomes more important still. The mere act of praying is no test of our relationship with God. It may be the routine of habit.

But to pray and receive clear answers, is the sure test and is the gracious point of our vital connection with Jesus Christ.

Dear God, please teach me to pray right. Our prayers can move Your arm that moves the universe. I praise Your name. Amen.

The Evidence of God's Existence

Answer me, O LORD, answer me, so these
people will know that You, O LORD, are God, and
that You are turning their hearts back again.
1 Kings 18:37

To God and to man, the answer to prayer is the all-important part of our praying. The answer to prayer, direct and unmistakable, is the evidence of God's existence.

It proves that God is interested in His creatures, and listens to them when they approach Him in prayer. There is no proof so clear and demonstrative that God exists than answered prayer.

The answer to prayer is the part of prayer that glorifies God. Unanswered prayers leave the praying ones in darkness and carry no conviction to the unbeliever. Answer to prayer is the convincing proof of a right relationship with God.

Father, Elijah's prayer is also my prayer today. Answer me, O LORD, so that the people will know that You are God, and that You are turning their hearts back again. In Jesus' name. Amen.

December 27

The Convincing Proof

*"Father, I thank You that You have heard Me.
I knew that You always hear Me, but I said
this for the benefit of the people standing here,
that they may believe that You sent Me."*
John 11:41-42

It is not the act or the attitude of praying that gives effectiveness to prayer. It is not the kneeling of the body before God or the exquisite beauty and poetry of our prayers that do the deed.

Not one or all of these are the things that glorify God. It is the answer that brings glory to His name. Answer to prayer is the living proof of our right relationship with God. Jesus said these words at the grave of Lazarus. The answer to His prayer was the proof of His mission from God.

Like Jesus I pray, "Father, I thank You that You have heard me. I know that You always hear me." Amen.

December 28

God Answers Prayers

Now I know that you are a man of God.
1 Kings 17:24

He is highest in the favor of God who has the readiest access and the greatest number of answers to prayer from God.

We have been nurturing a false faith and hiding the shame of our loss and inability to pray by the false, comforting plea that God does not answer directly or objectively, but indirectly and subjectively. Or we have comforted and nurtured our spiritual laziness by saying that it is not God's will to give it to us.

Faith teaches God's praying people that it is God's will to answer prayer. God answers all prayers and every prayer of His children who truly pray.

Through faith, Your children can be sure of Your answers to their prayers. Thank You, God, for Your loving goodness. Amen.

December 29

The Mark of God

Praise be to the God and Father of our Lord
Jesus Christ, who has blessed us in the heavenly
realms with every spiritual blessing in Christ.
Ephesians 1:3

It is by these answered prayers that human nature is enriched. Answered prayer brings us into constant, conscious communion with God, awakens and enlarges gratitude, and excites the melody and lofty inspiration of praise.

Answered prayer is the mark of God in our praying. It is the exchange with heaven, and establishes and realizes a relationship with God.

We give our prayers in exchange for the divine blessing. God accepts our prayers through the atoning blood and gives Himself, His presence, and His grace in return.

come before You with prayers of praise, Father. I want to thank You for all the blessings and goodness You bestow on us. I pray for forgiveness of my sins. Amen.

God's Truth

Do you show contempt for the riches of His kindness, tolerance and patience, not realizing that God's kindness leads you toward repentance?
Romans 2:4

God holds all good in His hands. That good comes to us through our Lord Jesus Christ, only because of His atoning sacrifice and by asking it in His name.

God is so much involved in prayer and hearing and answering that all His attributes and His whole being are centered in that great fact. It distinguishes Him as wonderfully good, and powerfully attractive in His nature.

God's truthfulness is at stake in the engagements to answer prayer. His wisdom, His truth, and His goodness are involved. God is Truth – and He always answers the prayers of His children who earnestly seek His name.

Father God, I know that if I ask anything in Your name You will provide for us. You are Truth. You always keep Your promises. May Your name be exalted over all the earth. Amen.

December 31